MACROSHIFT

THE OFFICIAL REPORT OF THE CLUB OF BUDAPEST

MACROSHIFT

NAVIGATING THE TRANSFORMATION TO A SUSTAINABLE WORLD

ERVIN LASZLO

FOREWORD BY ARTHUR C. CLARKE

BERRETT-KOEHLER PUBLISHERS, INC.
San Francisco

Portions of this book were previously published in *Third Millennium: the Challenge and the Vision*. Gaia Books, London, 1996, and *Macroshift: Creating the Future in the Early 21st Century* to Excel, San Jose, New York, Lincoln, and Shanghai, 2000

Berrett-Koehler Publishers, Inc.
235 Montgomery Street, Suite 650
San Francisco, CA 94104-2916
Tel: (415) 288-0260 Fax: (415) 362-2512 www.bkconnection.com

Ordering Information
Quantity sales. Special discounts are available on quantity purchases by corporations, associations, and others. For details, contact the "Special Sales Department" at the Berrett-Koehler address above.
Individual sales. Berrett-Koehler publications are available through most bookstores. They can also be ordered direct from Berrett-Koehler: Tel: (800) 929-2929; Fax: (802) 864-7626; www.bkconnection.com
Orders for college textbook/course adoption use. Please contact Berrett-Koehler: Tel: (800) 929-2929; Fax: (802) 864-7626.
Orders by U.S. trade bookstores and wholesalers. Please contact Publishers Group West, 1700 Fourth Street, Berkeley, CA 94710. Tel: (510) 528-1444; Fax: (510) 528-3444.

Printed in the United States of America

Library of Congress Cataloging-in-Publication Data
Ervin Laszlo, 1932–
    Macroshift : navigating the transformation to a sustainable world / Ervin Laszlo ; foreword by Arthur C. Clarke.
        p. cm.
    Includes bibliographical references and index.
    ISBN 1-57675-163-5
    1. Sustainable development—Mathematical models. 2. Globalization. I. Title
HC79.E2 .L375 2001
306.3—dc21   2001025658

First Edition

07 06 05 04 03 02 01   10 9 8 7 6 5 4 3 2 1

Interior Design: Gopa Design & Illustration   Proofreader: Stewart Burns
Copy Editor: Kay Mikel, WordWorks   Indexer: Paula C. Durbin-Westby
Production: Linda Jupiter, Jupiter Productions

for Christopher and Alexander

macroshift navigators of excellence

with pride and affection

~

The Club of Budapest, founded in 1993 by Ervin Laszlo, is an informal association of ethical globally as well as locally active opinion leaders in various fields of art, science, religion, and culture, dedicated to our common future. Its members include the Dalai Lama, Václav Havel, Mikhail Gorbachev, Desmond Tutu, Elie Wiesel, Peter Ustinov, Peter Gabriel, and young and creative people in many parts of the world. They place their names and energy into the service of what they consider the crucial mission of our time: *catalyzing the emergence of adapted vision and values in society by evolving our individual and collective consciousness.*

Contents

Foreword by Arthur C. Clarke

ANYONE WHO ATTEMPTS to write about the future should take warning from all the failures of the past. Even in the restricted field of technology, which is the only one where any kind of forecasting is possible, success has been very limited. And in geopolitical matters, it has been virtually nonexistent: did anyone predict the events of the last decade in Europe? So in this book, Ervin Laszlo, scientist, and founder and president of the Club of Budapest, makes a vital point: the future is not to be forecast, but created. What we do today will decide the shape of things tomorrow. Especially the way we perceive the challenges that await us, and the vision we develop for coping with them. His book furnishes essential guidelines for creating a positive scenario for our common future: for the new thinking and acting that this calls for.

I leave until later Laszlo's ideas, insights and injunctions—I begin by addressing the questions of engineering hardware, the area closest to my interests. Here, too, some of the warnings issued by Laszlo are relevant: for example, against obeying the technological imperative. Not all things that can be produced should, evidently, actually be produced. But there are many fascinating things that we can, and probably will, produce, and these deserve to be thought about.

The past record of technological forecasting is not encouraging. The failures of people to forecast the developments that awaited them fall into two categories: the hopelessly pessimistic and the overly optimistic. This may be because our logical processes are linear, whereas the real world obeys nonlinear processes, often with exponential laws. Thus we tend to exaggerate what can be done in the short run but hopelessly underestimate ultimate possibilities. Here are some of my favorite examples of this phenomenon.

When the news of Alexander Graham Bell's invention reached Britain, the Engineer-in-Chief of the Post Office exclaimed loftily: "The Americans have need of the telephone—but we do not. We have plenty of messenger boys." That is what I call a failure of imagination. Here, in contrast, is a failure of nerve, based on the same example. When the mayor of a certain American city heard about the telephone, he was wildly enthusiastic. "I can see the time," he exclaimed, "when every city will have one." What would he have thought, could he have known that one day many individuals would have half a dozen. . . .

Quite recently I came across another example of a comic failure, by a man determined not to be outguessed by the future. Around the end of the last century, the president of the Carriage Builders Association of Great Britain lectured his fellows on the subject of the newly invented motor car. "Anyone would be a fool," he said, "who denied that the motor car has an important future. But he would be an even bigger fool if he suggested that it would have any impact on the horse and carriage trade."

However, I cannot leave the subject of technological prediction without quoting from Norman Augustine, CEO of Martin Marietta and author of the wise and witty Augustine's Laws. He recently pointed to what he called "Coolidge's revenge," due around 2020. Apparently, when Calvin's administration was presented with an estimate of some $25,000 for the purchase of a dozen airplanes, the President asked testily, "Why can't they buy one—and let the aviators take turns flying it?" Well, Norm has calculated that, extrapolating the present rising cost of aircraft and electronics, in the twenty-first century the U.S. budget will indeed be able to afford just one airplane!

As everyone knows, we are now in the midst of one of the greatest technological revolutions in history, and if the bifurcations in the area of economy, ecology, and politics outlined in this report are adequately managed, the end will be nowhere in sight. Who could have imagined that something the size of a fingernail, constructed by technology inconceivable only a few decades ago, could change the face of commerce, industry, and everyday human life? Although we science fiction writers assumed that computers would play an important role in the future (Hi there, HAL!), nobody dreamed that one day the world population of computers would exceed that of human beings.

We are now approaching a time, for better or for worse, when we will be able to do anything that does not defy the laws of physics—and, especially after reading this report's review of the insights from the new physics, it may well turn out that we don't know those laws as well as we thought.

Obviously, many things are possible, but not all are desirable, *vide* the argument over human cloning, which I am not competent to discuss (though I suspect it will be taken for granted by our grandchildren, and they will wonder what all the fuss was about). I will stick to the engineering sciences, and here are some of my guesses in this area.

1. Discovery of revolutionary new power sources, possibly based on zero-point energy or quantum fluctuations. The zero-point field of the quantum vacuum, as Laszlo points out, emerges as one of the most crucial elements of the universe, and it may hold a number of surprises in the near future. This series of developments started a decade ago with the "Cold Fusion" caper and has now extended to quantum field physics. I am 99 percent sure that the end of the fossil fuel/nuclear age is now in sight, with awesome political and economic consequences—as well as some very desirable ones, such as ending the current threat of global warming and pollution.

2. Development of super-strength materials (e.g., carbon nanotubes) which will impact transportation, building construction—and especially space travel, by reducing the structural mass of space vehicles to a fraction of its present value.

This may lead to the construction of "space elevators" and orbital towers (see *3001: The Final Odyssey* for details). However, I am concerned about the danger of collision with the multitude of satellites below geostationary orbit; they may have to be banned. In any case, they will be unnecessary when we have permanent structures reaching thousands of kilometers out into space.

3. A "Space Drive," long the dream of science fiction writers—something to replace the noisy, inefficient, and downright dangerous rocket. There are a number of hints in rather far-out physics as to how such a device might operate, and I am happy to see that some scientists are working on them. When they are perfected, they will open up the Solar System, as sailing ships opened up this planet during the First Millennium.

4. Contact/detection of extraterrestrials: no one can predict when this will happen, but I would be surprised if it does not occur during the next few decades, as our technologies in this direction are developing rapidly. The recent excitement over putative Mars microbes indicates the interest this subject arouses in the public mind. Unfortunately, it has been confused with UFO and alien abduction nonsense—part of the pathology of the usual "millennium myths."

5. This is the Bad News. We now realize (especially after Shoe-maker-Levy's spectacular impact on Jupiter) that we live in a dangerous neighborhood. Ask the dinosaurs, if you can find one. Although the statistics are being vigorously disputed, few would deny that—next Wednesday, or a thousand years hence—a Near Earth Object (comet or asteroid) will cause catastrophic damage somewhere on this planet. The very least we should do is to initiate a survey of potentially dangerous NEOs, and Project SPACEGUARD (which I suggested in *Rendezvous with Rama* more than twenty years ago) is being established to promote this. What we should do if we see a Big Dumb Rock heading this way is a question that already has dozens of answers; some day, we will have to choose one of them.

At this point, perhaps I should obey Shelley's injunction:

> Cease—drain not to its dregs the urn
> Of bitter prophecy!

Yet, although prophecy is no doubt the most convenient way to cope with the future, it is not the only way. J. D. Bernal's *The World, the Flesh and the Devil*, one of the best books on foreseeing the future ever written, opens with the striking phrase: "There are two futures, the future of Desire and the future of Fate, and man's reason has never learnt to separate them." The future of Fate will not be disclosed until it unfolds, but reason, as exposed in this book, tells us that the future of Desire can be crucial to its unfolding. To quote another British poet, Robert Bridges, successful living depends upon the "masterful administration of the unforeseen." Such administration is now, in the midst of the civilizational change Laszlo calls "macroshift," important as never before. We must catch up with the world our technological genius has created—update the way we perceive it, the way we value it, and the way we act in it. Fortunately this is not a mere theoretical exercise, for the outcome of a macroshift is sensitive to changes in our perceptions and behaviors.

It is here, at the critical chaos-leap of the macroshift that the Future of Fate and the Future of Desire intersect—where desire, transformed into the masterful administration of the unforeseen, makes for a selection between a scenario of breakdown and a scenario of breakthrough. I leave the reader with this report of the Club of Budapest to see how the seeming paradox between unforeseeability and conscious choice can be resolved—how today's macroshift can be purposively and effectively navigated.

It is just as well that the real future has to be created and not just foreseen—for if we could know it, what would be the point of living?

Preface

IN THE OPENING YEARS of the twenty-first century we are launched on a process of profound and irreversible transformation. The problems and crises we have been experiencing in recent years are driving past the tolerance threshold of nationally based industrial societies toward a borderless world where information is the key resource and communication the key to making use of it.

This process is more profound than the much discussed globalization of local, regional, and national economies through technology, finance, communication, and trade. Today's transformation is not just economic, it is a *civilizational* process. It is part of a long-term evolutionary trend that drives toward the progressive integration of different groups, economies, societies, and cultures in systems that embrace ever more people and ever larger territories. This process has now reached the limits of the planet; it is "globalizing." Economic globalization is part of it—but only a part.

The message of this book is that ours is an era of total-range evolutionary transformation that could, and ultimately will, go beyond economic globalization to pave the way toward a shift in civilization. This is an era of *macroshift*: a shift that is all-embracing, rapid, and irreversible, extending to the far corners of the globe and involving practically all aspects of life. It is driven by technology, but the stresses and conflicts it creates do not have purely technological solutions. Because of the rapid and unreflective exploitation of our technological genius, we live and act in conditions for which we are poorly prepared. Established values, vision, and behavior have become useless and even dangerous. We must update the way we perceive our world and the way we value it so that we would change the way we act in it. This, in the final count, is the crux of the matter.

Trying to reverse a macroshift would be quixotic—a wasted effort. But this is not to say that we can sit with folded hands, waiting for the macroshift to take its course. A macroshift's unfolding is never predetermined: it is sensitive to human perceptions, values, and actions. Like a giant supertanker in turbulent waters, a macroshift cannot be simply steered, but with foresight and understanding it can be navigated. Understanding this possibility and acting on it is important, for today's macroshift harbors great promise as well as grave danger. It could lead to a more humane and sustainable civilization or to a series of crises that lead to catastrophe. If we are to avert its dangers and realize its promise, we must see this process for what it is and act purposefully to steer toward a humanly desirable outcome.

This is not utopia: it can be done. The present report aims to provide that modicum of insight and information which is the basic precondition for navigating the macroshift in ways that are both effective and ethical.

Acknowledgments

In writing this report an invaluable resource has been the materials and comments I received from friends and colleagues in recent months as well as over the years. I cannot thank everyone individually who has helped me to evolve and formulate my views, but if I am to choose a few individuals whose collaboration has been especially memorable I would name Richard Falk and Saul Mendlowitz at Princeton's Center of International Studies, Aurelio Peccei and Alexander King at the Club of Rome, Davidson Nicol and Joel Kurtzman at the United Nations Institute for Training and Research, Kinhide Mushakoji at the United Nations University, Iván Vitányi and Mária Sági at Eurocircon, Federico Mayor at UNESCO, and Thomas Druyen, Fiona Montagu, Mária Sági, and

Peter Ustinov at the Club of Budapest. Historian of civilization Alastair Taylor provided me with the historical and conceptual background for the evolution of worldviews from Mythos to Logos, and Alfonso ("Monty") Montuori of the California Institute of Integral Studies and Christopher Laszlo of the Innov-Ethics Group put at my disposal valuable materials on the relevance of the macroshift to business.

The enthusiasm, expertise, and unfailing dedication of the entire editorial team led by Steve Piersanti at Berrett-Koehler proved to be a further priceless resource. My heartfelt thanks go to them all, and also to my wife Carita, who gave me the time and the peace of mind to think and write in our converted farmhouse in Tuscany during that remarkably intense but exciting period when the ideas for this book found their way from sketches on the back of some envelopes to their present shape in print.

The factual basis for this report—the wide variety of "hard" data concerning the state of the world, and the "softer" but just as relevant data on the state of people's mind as they contemplate the state of the world—has been furnished by the many organizations, national and international, governmental and nongovernmental, with which it has been my good fortune to be associated over the years: first at Princeton, then at the United Nations, and currently through the Club of Budapest. Rather than listing each source individually, I take this opportunity to acknowledge my indebtedness to this precious stream of information that has not ceased to reach my hands day after day, year after year. Of course, the interpretation of this information I am giving is my own: it is based on my decades-long work in the systems and evolutionary sciences.

The scientifically inclined reader will find a detailed bibliography of the sources for my review of cutting-edge science, together with suggestions for further reading, following the Postscript.

Ervin Laszlo
Montescudaio, Pisa (Italy)
January/February 2001

PART ONE

World in Macroshift

~

W E LIVE IN AN ERA OF DEEP-SEATED TRANSFORMATION—a shift in civilization. Its signs and manifestations are all around us. While globalization is integrating production, trade, finance, and communication, it is producing a social and ecological backlash characterized by regional unemployment, widening income gaps, and environmental degradation. The benefits of economic growth, for long the main indicator of progress, are becoming more and more concentrated. Hundreds of millions live at a higher material standard of living, but thousands of millions are pressed into abject poverty, living in shantytowns and urban ghettos in the shadows of ostentatious affluence. This is socially and politically explosive: it fuels resentment and revolt and provokes massive migration from the countryside to the cities, and from the poorer to the richer regions. In such conditions organized crime, already growing into a global enterprise, finds fertile ground with a gamut of activities ranging from information fraud to traffic in arms, drugs, and human organs.

The application of new technologies, another indicator of progress, is a two-edged sword. Nuclear power promises an unlimited supply of commercial energy, but disposal of nuclear wastes and decommissioning aging reactors pose unsolved puzzles, and the specter of nuclear meltdown, whether due to technical accident or intentional terrorism, remains unchallenged. Genetic engineering has a fabulous potential for creating virus-resistant and protein-rich plants, improved breeds of animals, vast supplies of animal proteins, and microorganisms capable of producing proteins and hormones and improving photosynthesis. But genetic engineering can also produce lethal biological weapons and pathogenic microorganisms, destroy the diversity and the balance of nature, and create abnormal—and abnormally aggressive—insects and animals.

Our information technologies could create a globally interact-ing yet locally diverse civilization, enabling all people to be linked whatever their culture and ethnic or national origin. But if these networks remain dominated by the power groups that brought them into being, they will serve only the narrowly focused interests of a small minority of people and marginalize the rest. If the Inter-net, television, and the electronic and print media become further commercialized, these media will cater to the demands of those who have the means to enter the global marketplace rather than giving voice to all people. Worse than that, the cyberspace of telecommunications could become a new medium for information warfare, intolerant cultural influences, pornography, and crime.

But the macroshift today harbors not only danger; it is also the cradle of opportunity. Our globalized technological civilization could break down in chaos and anarchy—or it could break through to a more humane and sustainable world. The choice between these possibilities will not be made by applying technological fixes or implementing strategies based on the same kind of thinking that created today's unsustainabilities. As this report will show, to master our destiny we need new thinking, new values—a new consciousness.

In this opening Part we first review the nature and dynamics of macroshifts, and then describe how they came about in history and how the one we now experience is unfolding in the contemporary world. We then outline the factors that influence its unfolding and show that they are not written in the stars but depend on the evolution of our values and behaviors. The oft-neglected value-sensitivity of macroshifts is what opens for us a real opportunity to choose our destiny—and the unprecedented responsibility to choose it wisely.

I

What Is a Macroshift?

OUR FUTURE—THE FUTURE OF HUMANKIND—will be decided by the outcome of today's macroshift. But what is a macroshift? If our future depends on its outcome, and especially if we can do something about influencing this outcome, understanding today's macroshift is important. Indeed, it is uniquely and decisively important.

Let us begin at the beginning. The most basic question we can ask about our future is whether we can know it. Very different answers can be given to this simple question. We may shrug and say, "I don't know and don't really care—I just take one thing at a time and the future will take care of itself." Or we may say that there are no answers to this question, or at least none that we could give with any measure of confidence. Prediction, after all, is a difficult business—especially, as the saying goes, when it is about the future. But we can also say that there are reasonable and credible ways to answer questions about our future by looking at the present. Just as the present has emerged out of the past, the future is likely to follow from conditions in the present. After all, where we are going has much to do with where we have been.

Indifference and skepticism are widespread attitudes, but they are not helpful when the world is changing before our eyes. If you choose to opt out of taking real responsibility for the consequences of your actions because such consequences are said to be unforeseeable and, in any case, are none of your business, you may as well quit reading now. But if you believe, or at least are open to the possibility, that we can say something meaningful about where we are going and, even more, that we may have a real role in deciding it, then read on.

What is it, then, that we can say with a measure of confidence about the shape of things to come? The simplest and most common answer is that the future will follow from the present and will not be radically different from it. As the French saying goes, *plus ça change, plus c'est la même chose* (the more things change, the more they are the same). After all, we are dealing with humans and human nature, and these will be pretty much the same tomorrow as they are today. A more sophisticated variant of this popular view adds that long-term ongoing processes of today will introduce some measure of change and make some difference tomorrow. These processes are typically viewed as "trends." Trends, whether local or global, micro or mega, introduce a measure of difference: as trends unfold, there are more of some things and less of others. The world is still the same, only some people are better off and others worse.

This is the view typically held by futurists, forecasters, and trend analysts in general. A good example of this is the much-publicized report of the U.S. National Intelligence Council, *Global Trends 2015: A Dialogue about the Future with Nongovernment Experts* (Washington, DC 2000). The view of the world of 2015 that emerges in this nonclassified report is based on the unfolding of key trends, catalyzed by key drivers. The seven key trends and drivers are demographics, natural resources and environment, science and technology, the global economy and globalization, national and international governance, future conflict, and the role of the United States. The way these trends unfold under the impact of their drivers can produce four different futures: a future of inclusive globalization, another future of pernicious globalization, a future of regional competition, or a post-polar world. The main deciders are the effects of globalization—they can be positive or negative—and the level and management of the world's potential for interstate and interregional conflict.

When all these factors are taken into account, we get what the experts call "the optimistic scenario." In this perspective the world of 2015 is much like today's world except that some population segments (alas, a shrinking minority) are better off and other segments (a growing majority) are less well off. The global economy will continue to grow, although its path will be rocky and marked by sustained financial volatility and a widening economic divide.

Economic growth may be undone, however, by events such as a sustained financial crisis or a prolonged disruption of energy supplies. Other "discontinuities" may occur as well. Here is a short list of possible problems from the *Global Trends 2015* report:

- violent political upheavals due to a serious deterioration of living standards in the Middle East;

- the formation of an international terrorist coalition with anti-Western aims and access to high-tech weaponry;

- a global epidemic on the scale of HIV/AIDS;

- rapidly changing weather-patterns that inflict grave damage on human health and on economies;

- the antiglobalization movement growing until it becomes a threat to Western governmental and corporate interests; the emergence of a geo-strategic alliance (possibly by Russia, China, and India) aimed at counterbalancing the United States and Western influence;

- collapse of the alliance between the United States and Europe; or

- creation of a counterforce organization that could undermine the power of the International Monetary Fund and the World Trade Organization and thus the ability of the United States to exercise global economic leadership.

With all these uncertainties and discontinuities we are far from justifying the assumption that the future will be much like the present. It is anybody's guess whether the world of 2015 will be the same

kind of world as the world we live in today—or something quite
different.

> ∼ *Given the unsustainability of many trends and processes in*
> *today's world, the dynamic of development that will apply to our*
> *future is not the linear dynamic of classical extrapolation but the*
> *nonlinear chaos dynamic of complex-system evolution.* ∼

This dilemma highlights the limits of trend-based forecasting.
Trends unfold in time, but they can also break down and give rise
to new trends and new processes. After all, no trend operates in an
infinite environment; its unfolding has limits. These may be natural limits due to finite resources and supplies, or human and social
limits due to changing structures, values, and expectations. When
a major trend encounters such limits, the world has changed and a
new dynamic enters into play. Extrapolating existing trends does
not help us define this moment. We need to know what happens
precisely when a trend breaks down. This calls for deeper insight.
We must go beyond observing current trends and following their
expected path. We must know something about the developmental
dynamics of the system in which trends appear—and then disappear. Such knowledge is theoretical but it is cogent—and it is available. It comes from the theory of complex systems, popularly
known as "chaos theory."

Given the unsustainability of many trends and processes in
today's world, the dynamic of development that will apply to our
future is not the linear dynamic of classical extrapolation but the
nonlinear chaos dynamic of complex-system evolution. Few would
deny that current trends are building toward some critical threshold—toward some of the famous (or infamous) "planetary limits"
that in the 1970s and 1980s were said to be the limits to growth.
Whether they are limits to growth altogether is questionable, but
they are clearly limits to the kind of growth that is occurring today.

As we move toward these limits, we are approaching a period of instability. It will mark the deflection or disappearance of some of the current trends and the appearance of others. This is not unusual: systems and chaos theory tell us that the evolution of complex systems always involves alternating periods of stability and instability, continuity and discontinuity, order and chaos. We are at the threshold of a period of instability today—a period of chaos.

Evolution through Macroshifts

> ⌁ *A macroshift is a bifurcation in the evolutionary dynamic of a society—in our interacting and interdependent world it is a bifurcation of human civilization in its quasi totality.* ⌁

Processes of rapid and fundamental change in complex systems are known as "bifurcations." The term, coming from the branch of physics known as nonequilibrium thermodynamics, has been popularized in chaos theory. It means that the hitherto continuous evolutionary path of a system forks off: thereafter the system evolves in a different way. Or it may not evolve at all: the system could also disappear, decomposing to its individually stable components. A macroshift is a bifurcation in the evolutionary dynamic of a society—in our interacting and interdependent world it is a bifurcation of human civilization in its quasi totality.

Of the variety of bifurcations known to systems and chaos theorists, the kind that interests us is the one called "catastrophic bifurcation." Here the system's relatively stable "point" and "periodic" attractors are joined by "chaotic" or "strange" attractors. These appear suddenly, as chaos theorists say, "out of the blue." They drive the system into a supersensitive state, the state of chaos. The chaotic state is not an unordered, random state but one where even immeasurably small fluctuations produce measurable, macroscopic effects.

These are the legendary "butterfly effects." (The story goes that if a monarch butterfly flaps its wings in California it creates a tiny air fluctuation that amplifies and amplifies and ends by creating a storm over Mongolia.)

The discovery of the butterfly effect is linked with the art of weather forecasting, having its roots in the shape assumed by the first chaotic attractor when it was discovered by U.S. meteorologist Edward Lorenz in the 1960s. When Lorenz attempted to computer-model the supersensitive evolution of the world's weather, he found a strange evolutionary path, consisting of two different trajectories joined together similarly to the wings of a butterfly. The slightest disturbance would shift the evolutionary trajectory of the world's weather from one of the wings to the other. The weather, it appears, is a system in a permanently chaotic state—a system permanently governed by chaotic attractors.

Subsequently a considerable variety of chaotic attractors have been discovered. They are applicable in some measure to all complex systems, above all to living systems. Living systems maintain themselves in the physically improbable state far from thermal and chemical equilibrium. They are remarkable systems. Living systems do not move toward equilibrium, as classical physical systems do, but maintain themselves in their improbable state by constantly replenishing the energies and matter they consume with fresh energies and matter obtained from their environment. (Physicists would say that they balance the positive entropy they produce by importing negative entropy.) In doing so the more complex variety of systems makes use of an additional factor: information. The human brain and nervous system, for example, is a complex information-processing system adapted through the mechanisms of genetic mutation and natural selection to perceive and select suitable sources of energy and matter in the organism's milieu; to enable the organism to ingest and absorb these energies; and to use them to fuel the organism's own life processes. These processes go on as long as human beings live; it makes us into open "negentropic" systems that self-maintain and self-organize in our ecological and social environment.

Humans as individual organisms are not alone in being self-maintaining and organizing open systems. The groups and systems humans form are also systems of this kind. Individuals are born, grow to maturity, and die, but the societies they form and the ecologies in which they participate continue to exist. The dynamic of complex-systems evolution applies also to these larger entities.

Human societies are complex systems made up of the relations of individually conscious humans to each other and to their environment. The presence of human mind and consciousness complicate the evolutionary dynamic of these systems. The evolution of natural systems usually can be described with differential equations that map the behavior of the systems in reference to the principal system constraints. This is not the case when it comes to human societies. Here the consciousness of the society's members influences the system's behavior, affecting the evolution of the system in a variety of unforeseen ways.

⌒ When a human society reaches the limits of its stability, it becomes supersensitive and is highly responsive to the smallest fluctuation. Then the system responds even to subtle changes in values, beliefs, worldviews, and aspirations. ⌒

In periods of relative stability the consciousness of individuals does not play a decisive role in society's evolution, but in periods of chaos it does. When a human society reaches the limits of its stability, it becomes supersensitive and is highly responsive to the smallest fluctuation. Then the system responds even to subtle changes in values, beliefs, worldviews, and aspirations.

A macroshift is a process of societal evolution in which encounter with the system's limits of stability initiates a bifurcation: an era of transformation. This is an era of unprecedented freedom to decide the system's future. The outcome of the "chaos leap" of a bifurcation is initially undecided. Selection from among a range of possible alternatives is ultimately decided by the nature of the "fluctuations" that occur either within that system or in its surroundings. In human societies these fluctuations can be consciously governed. As consumers and clients, as taxpayers and voters, and as public opinion holders, we create the kinds of fluctuations that will decide the outcome of our society's macroshift. If we are aware of this power in our hands, and if we have the will and the wisdom to make use of it, we can become conscious agents of our society's bifurcation—that is, masters of our own destiny.

FOUR PHASES OF A MACROSHIFT

1. The Trigger Phase

Innovations in "hard" technologies (tools, machines, operational systems) bring about greater efficiency in the manipulation of nature for human ends.

2. The Transformation Phase

Hard technology innovations irreversibly change social and environmental relations and bring about, successively,

◆ a higher level of resource production,

◆ faster growth of population,

◆ greater societal complexity, and

◆ a growing impact on the social and the natural environment.

3. The Critical (or "Chaos") Phase

Changed social and environmental relations put pressure on the established culture, placing into question time-honored values and worldviews and the ethics and ambitions associated with them. Society becomes chaotic in the chaos theory sense of the term. Society does not lack order but exhibits a subtle order that is extremely sensitive to fluctuations. The evolution of the dominant culture and consciousness—the way people's values, views and ethics respond and change—determine the outcome of the system's chaos leap (the way its developmental trajectory forks off).

4 (a). The Breakdown Phase

The values, worldviews, and ethics of a critical mass of people in society is resistant to change, or changes too slowly, and the established institutions are too rigid to allow for timely transformation. Social complexity, coupled with a degenerating environment, creates unmanageable stresses. The social order is exposed to a series of crises that soon degenerate into conflict and violence.

or

4 (b). The Breakthrough Phase

The mindset of a critical mass of people evolves in time, shifting the culture of society toward a better adapted mode. As these changes take hold, the improved social order—governed by more adapted values, worldviews, and associated ethics—establishes itself. The social system stabilizes itself in its changed conditions.

The four phases of a macroshift describe the dynamic of the evolutionary process in human societies. The first phase is the trigger phase. In this phase a set of technological innovations launches the macroshift (here "technology" is understood in the broadest sense, as any tool, technique, or means whereby humans interact with each other and with nature). Of the many technological innovations that surface in society, only the ones that help people do what they want to do with greater ease and less investment of time, energy, and money are implemented. These innovations amplify the power of muscles to move and transform matter, they extend the power of the eye to see and the ear to hear, and they enlarge the power of the brain to register and compute information. As a rule, these innovations are implemented without much regard for their consequences; the innovators think only of greater efficiency and effectiveness in carrying out the tasks and projects they want to see carried out.

In the second phase of a macroshift, the transformation phase, the proliferation of new technologies goes beyond the ability of the existing structures and institutions to manage and control. Those who own the new technologies work more effectively, but in doing so they create instability. More resources are produced, both by a more effective exploitation of the already exploited resources and by opening up new resources (for example, coal in addition to wood, then oil in addition to coal). The availability of a larger quantity and a wider variety of resources enables more people to produce and to consume. As a result, the population grows. But a larger population using more, and more kinds of, resources cannot make do with the kind of structures that served life based on simpler and more limited resources. There is a need for special skills and special purpose organizational structures. As these are developed, the complexity of society grows, together with its population and its resource base. In the absence of a suitable change in the dominant culture, social and political stability suffer.

Society grows beyond its traditional bounds, into an international and intercultural dimension. A more complex society with more people using more resources puts previously separate people not only into contact with each other but also into dependence on one another. As intercommunity trade develops, the scope of social interaction expands, and there is more intense exchange between diverse peoples and cultures. There is a corresponding pressure on society's traditional structures and relations of power. The established institutions are under stress, and new ways of living, administering communities, and doing business are required. Some people come up with the new ways and reap the benefits; others fail to come along. Social structures tend to polarize into rich and poor, powerful and marginalized segments.

Societal expansion and increased complexity have another unexpected consequence: they place a greater load on the life supporting environment. Nature suffers in unforeseen ways: forests fail to regenerate, soils are impoverished, water tables are lowered and become polluted, and the very air over densely inhabited areas becomes unhealthy.

⁓ The macroshift moves toward a successful conclusion if, and only if, a critical mass of people in society evolve their mindset: if they generate and embrace values, worldviews, and ethics that mesh with the conditions that were inadvertently spawned by the technological innovations of their predecessors. ⁓

In the third phase of the macroshift, the critical phase, society's transformation builds toward a crucial threshold. Expansion and integration combined with environmental degeneration produce unexpected consequences that disorient people and overload the administrative and control capacity of institutions. Society enters a period of social and cultural chaos, with some people holding to established values and swearing by tried and tested methods while a growing number look for alternatives.

The macroshift moves toward a successful conclusion if, and only if, a critical mass of people in society evolve their mindset. They must generate and embrace values, worldviews, and ethics that mesh with the conditions that were inadvertently spawned by the technological innovations of their predecessors. How soon and indeed whether a critical mass evolves its values, worldviews, and consciousness is not written in the stars. It depends on the creativity of the people and the flexibility of the dominant institutions. These vary from age to age, culture to culture, and society to society.

In any event, when the critical threshold of a chaos leap is breached, a fourth phase gets under way. It brings either breakdown or breakthrough. Society either restabilizes, thanks to the evolution of a more adapted mindset, or heads toward crises and breakdown.

The insight emerging from this four-phase dynamic is simple and straightforward. Macroshifts are triggered by technological innovations that destabilize the established structures and institutions of society. More adapted structures and institutions await the surfacing of a more adapted mindset in the bulk of the population. Consequently, a macroshift is a transformation of civilization in which technology is the driver and the values and consciousness of a critical mass of people the decider.

2

Macroshifts Past and Present

W INSTON CHURCHILL ONCE REMARKED, "the further backward you look, the further forward you can see." Since we want to see far enough forward to know what happens—or rather, what *can* happen—when today's macroshift enters the critical phase, we begin by looking backward: at macroshifts in history. We do not expect to see the events of history repeat themselves, but the dynamic that drives history could well repeat. That will have much to teach us. Because George Santayana's oft-quoted saying is not entirely mistaken: "those who ignore the past are obliged to repeat it." Repeating, if not the macroshifts of the past, then the way people related to those macroshifts, could be dangerous. Indeed, it could spell the very end of human civilization.

Macroshifts in History

Historian of civilization Alastair Taylor pointed out (first in Burbank and Taylor, *Civilizations Past and Present* and again in his latest work, *Time-Space Technics*) that ever since our forefathers evolved some form of culture and some form of social order, periodic shifts in their relations to each other and to nature were accompanied by corresponding shifts in their beliefs and worldviews. Together, these "objective" and "subjective" shifts produced integral civilizational shifts.

THE MACROSHIFT FROM MYTHOS TO THEOS

About a million years ago the earliest bands of five to eighty nomads, consisting of one or more extended families, spread from Africa into Eurasia. These Paleolithic people held territory in common and had an informal leadership based on personality, strength, and fighting skills. Everyone, including children, foraged for food, and adult males engaged in hunting. The technologies they used were simple but effective. They consisted of objects improvised as tools or as weapons, and later of the purposive fashioning of objects (such as hand axes) according to tradition. These served for hunting and warfare, for making and controlling fire, for adapting and building shelters, and for rites and rituals connected with birth, maturity, and death.

By 11,000 B.C., in the Fertile Crescent, the formerly verdant region extending from the Levant to Persia (now Iran), human groups had grown into tribes of several hundred living in fixed settlements. This was made possible by the concentration of resources such as wild cereals. In the larger and more complex human groups of this Neolithic Age, additional technologies came into use, including cultivating plants, husbanding animals, and weaving and pottery making.

The culture of our forebears underwent a corresponding shift. Neolithic people had a wealth of zoological and botanical knowledge, and were experts at some forms of agriculture and pastoralism. But their imagination did not stop at the limits of their everyday world; their worldview was embracing in its dimensions and animistic and spiritualistic in its substance. Spirit was not separated from matter, nor the real world from the dream world. The forces of nature were also the forces of the spirits embodied in objects, plants, animals, and people. The entire world had a sacred dimension. Forces outside and above humans acted in and on the world, having an impact on nature as well as on human communities. People viewed themselves as belonging to a dynamic universe, with seen and unseen forces and entities.

Time and space were part of the natural order. The present time was associated with local space, and the future was seen as a continuous recurrence of the rhythms experienced in the present. The seasons were known to follow each other, but there were no new seasons; all times had already been experienced.

Animism was joined with totemism—the belief that an object, animal, or plant serves as emblem of a family or clan and its ancestry—as well as with rituals and magic. Magic included socially adopted techniques for tapping the higher forces of the cosmos to help humans achieve the ends they desired. These communities had a high level of integration. The individual was an essential part of the clan or tribe, which in turn was embedded in nature and governed by cosmic forces. Nature and humans did not exist in separation, much less in opposition. Humans had empathy with all they encountered.

The varieties of "lithic" belief systems were suited to people's ways of life and their relations to nature. At the Paleolithic food-gathering and hunting-fishing stage, the male principle dominated, consistent with the survival priorities and needs of the times. Subsequently, at the agriculturally based Neolithic stage of food production, the female principle became dominant, reflecting the new relations of the herder and farmer to the soil and the Earth. Earth-oriented fecundity and fertility, sexual symbolism, and magical-religious rites were remarkably similar among widely separated peoples. They found analogous expression in the Old World in Asia and the Middle East and in the New World of the Meso-Americas.

The seemingly infinite endurance of stone-age societies came to an end when the gradual improvement of their tool-based technologies changed people's relations to nature. Neolithic people congregated primarily in major river valleys, where their use of large amounts of water in improved irrigation systems generated massive increments of crops. Metals such as copper and bronze came into use, new methods for measuring the boundaries of lands were discovered, and calendars for reckoning time and writing for recording and communicating messages were invented. This brought about increases in population and growth in the complexity of social organization and created a greater load on the environment. In some regions of the Fertile Crescent, such as Sumer, trees were chopped down, soils overworked, and the climate became arid. But Neolithic communities fanned out, working vaster lands and drawing on the resources of a larger environment. Many villages grew into towns. In time some became incorporated as empires with extended administrative and power structures. A new elite came to inhabit the urban centers. The tribal circle of stone-age communities yielded to the stratified pyramid of the formally organized state characterized by a hierarchical structure and strict discipline. Such were the archaic empires that appeared in Babylonia and in Egypt, China, and India.

The new structures and orders mirrored, and in turn reinforced, the transformation of people's values and worldviews. As fresh emphasis was placed on male dominance, in line with higher socio-economic stratification, the Earth Mother was subordinated to "sky gods." Territorial rights came to dominate over traditional kinship ties, reflecting increased concern with individual and communal property and a more complex division of labor.

The emerging worldview accounted for the origins and justified the orders of the archaic civilizations. The beginning of the world was thought to be rooted in the emergence of order out of chaos, followed by a further distillation of order in the heavens, mirrored by emerging orders on Earth. The cosmos was viewed as an organic polity in its own right, possessing both sovereignty and power, and maintaining order and harmony throughout the reaches of the universe. Its powers had been created and were wielded by a supreme being, or else by a hierarchy of deities.

People looked to the heavens rather than to the earth for guidance. They were ruled by kings who claimed divine descent and were related to the celestial spheres populated by a pantheon of deities. The celestial orders above called for a theocratic order below. On the principle "as above, so below," human life expanded into a network of relations that extended from the deepest layers of living and nonliving nature to the highest spheres of the heavens.

In theocratic societies kings ruling by divine fiat embodied and legitimized the exercise of celestially authorized power. Cosmic godship and earthly kingship were united in the intent to maintain an embracing order where the order below reflected the order people believed to reign above. The supreme aim was the maintenance of the essential balance of the universe through a social order rooted in cosmic principles. These elements, but with local variations, appeared in ancient Egypt, Mesopotamia, India, and China, as well as in Meso-America. They consolidated the centuries-long macroshift from the Stone Age of *Mythos* to the archaic world of *Theos*.

THE MACROSHIFT FROM THEOS TO LOGOS

Even though it was bolstered and underpinned by an elaborate and entrenched culture complete with an enshrined worldview, values, and ethical code, the world of Theos yielded in time to another world, dominated by different beliefs and guided by different values.

This macroshift originated with the introduction of iron technology in the theocratic civilizations. In the second millennium B.C. Indo-European peoples equipped with this technology swept out of Central Asia in several directions. Some came through the Khyber Pass into India, where they put an end to the already enfeebled Indus civilization. Others moved southwest into what was then Persia, and still others penetrated to the Black Sea and Eastern Europe, migrating north along the Volga or west along the Danube and the Rhine. Still others settled on the northern coast of the Mediterranean, in the Greek and Italian peninsulas. In time they gave rise to the Greek city-states and to the Greco-Roman civilization. The former extended, under Alexander, to the limits of the then known world, and the latter, under the Emperors, stretched from Britain to the Tigris-Euphrates and the Sahara.

The technologies of these civilizations triggered change in their social structure, and these changes were reflected in corresponding

shifts in values and beliefs. In classical Hellas the pioneers of the
new worldview were the great nature-philosophers. They replaced
mythical concepts with theories based on observation and elaborated by reasoning. The pre-Socratic philosophers evolved the
"heroic mind," present in Homer and the early epics, into the
visionary and the theoretical mind, in a process that culminated
with Socrates in the rational mind that was then epitomized by
Plato and Aristotle. *Logos* became the central concept: it was at the
heart of philosophy as well as of religion. Together with the concept
of quantitative measure, *metron*, it provided Western civilization
with the intellectual foundation upon which it was to build for
nearly two and a half millennia.

Logos, as embodied by classical Greco-Roman civilization, was
not a purely quantitative worldview, devoid of qualitative elements.
Humans, and to some extent all creatures, had special worth or
virtue, *arēte*, not accountable in terms of quantitative properties
alone. The combination of *logos* and *metron* with *arēte* constituted a
worldview, an ethic, and a system of values that was altogether different from the Theos civilization of the archaic empires. Man was
the measure, and the unfolding of human potentials was the goal.
This basic notion, with many sophisticated variants, came to flower
in the philosophical systems of the Hellenic thinkers and found
application in the organization of Greek city-states. Many of its
elements were carried over into Roman civilization, endowed with
a pragmatic orientation keyed to the maintenance of order through
the orderly exercise of power.

After the fall of the Western Empire and the founding of the
Eastern, Byzantine Empire in A.D. 476, a further shift occurred in
the ways of life, consciousness, and organization of European societies. The rise of Christianity modified the classical culture of
Logos. Christianity added to the traditional concepts a divine
source believed to be the world's creator, prime mover, as well as
ultimate judge. Logos came to be embodied in the Holy Trinity
and incarnated in man, God's creation. Medieval Logos, whose
principal elements were elaborated by Augustine and Thomas

Aquinas, was dominant in European civilization until the advent of the modern age.

The reign of medieval Logos was not eternal, however. A further shift occurred in the mindset of Europe in the sixteenth and seventeenth centuries. It built on the rationality of the Greeks, borrowed and elaborated by the Romans, that was conserved in medieval fiefdoms and princedoms notwithstanding the addition of Christian elements. It found expression outside medieval monasteries in the creation and use of mechanical devices such as clocks, windmills, watermills, animal-drawn agricultural implements and horse-drawn carriages.

In the seventeenth century Europe's mechanically colored Logos culminated in the concept of the world as a giant machine, which was elaborated by Giordano Bruno and Galileo Galilei. Newton's mathematical demonstration of the universality of the laws of motion confirmed Galileo's pioneering insights and provided a basis for embracing a world concept that became the hallmark of the modern age. The new concept took hold on the Continent as well as on the British Isles. It accounted for the behavior of bodies on Earth, the same as the movement of the heavens, by mechanical principles. The universe was a divinely designed clockwork that was set in motion by a prime mover and then ran harmoniously through all eternity. It was believed to operate according to strict laws of nature. A knowledge of these laws was said to enable the rational mind to know all things past, present and future. The place of God in this system was restricted to being its "prime mover," and as Laplace is reputed to have commented to Napoleon, God was a hypothesis for which there was no longer any need.

At first there was open conflict between the medieval Logos imposed by the Church and the mechanistic and naturalistic Logos supported by the rise of modern science. But inquiry independent of religious dogma soon took off outside the monastic walls. Church and science learned to coexist, and an accommodation was reached. The Church claimed for itself the domain of "moral philosophy" (which embraced what later came to be called the social sciences and the humanities), and science had the field of "natural philosophy" (which corresponded to the contemporary concept of natural science). This accommodation was a socially useful development, because the conception of the natural world as a giant and reliable mechanism was a counterweight to the disunity of the warring princedoms. It offered a more secure orientation for human aspirations than what Galileo called "the passions that divide the minds of men."

In nineteenth-century Europe and America, the scientific worldview became the dominant feature of civilization. Darwin's theory of evolution completed the mechanistic worldview of Newtonian physics; it accounted for the evolution of life from simple origins through the basic mechanism of random mutations exposed to the test of natural selection. The worldview that emerged was "purified" and "objective," believed to be free of subjective and emotional elements. In the influential heritage of French philosopher René Descartes, human consciousness was considered the sole indubitable reality (*cogito ergo sum*—I think therefore I am); the natural world, though not known with absolute certainty, was pure "extension," without mind and spirit. It followed that conscious humans were free to exploit nonconscious nature for purposes of their own. In the words of Francis Bacon, they were free to wrest nature's secrets from her bosom for their own benefit.

This was the mechanistic-materialistic Logos that spread in the eighteenth and nineteenth centuries from Europe to America, and in the twentieth century from America to the rest of the world.

The Macroshift Today

The age of Mythos was dominated by mythical consciousness; the age of Theos by theistic consciousness; and the modern age by a mechanistically rational Logos consciousness. These mindsets were useful and functional in their time. Indeed, the reason human culture and civilization continued to exist and evolve is because more adapted forms of consciousness arose from time to time. Of course, they did not arise everywhere and in all times: countless civilizations failed to survive, victims of changing conditions to which they could not adapt. This failure is not one we can contemplate today.

> ∼ *If our Logos-dominated civilization fails to adapt to the conditions it has itself created, the entire economic and political structure of our world will come crashing down.* ∼

It has become imperative to update the thinking, the values, and the consciousness of modern-age Logos. To appreciate the full import of this imperative, let's review the four phases of the macroshift we are currently living through—the macroshift from national industrial societies toward a globally interdependent yet locally diverse world.

1. The Build Up, 1860–1960

Innovations in "hard" technologies (tools, machines, operational systems) create significant changes in the way people live and work in the name of creating greater efficiency in the manipulation of people, resources, and nature for human ends.

This was the trigger phase of the bifurcation.

2. Globalization, 1960 to the Present

Hard technology innovations irreversibly transform social and environmental relations and bring about, successively,

- a higher level of resource production,
- faster growth in the population,
- growing societal complexity, and
- a growing impact on the natural environment.

This was—and is—the transformation phase that continues to this day.

3. The Decisive Epoch, 2001–2010

New conditions in society and the environment stress the dominant social order. They place in question the established values, worldviews, ethics, and aspirations. Society enters a period of ferment, approximating the chaos that comes about when complex systems reach the limits of their stability. It is the flexibility and creativity of the people that creates that subtle but all-important "fluctuation" that decides which of the available evolutionary paths the macroshift will then follow.

This is the critical (or "chaos") phase we are now entering.

4 (a). The Doomsday Scenario, 2010 and Beyond

People's values, worldviews, ethics, and ambitions prove to be resistant to change; the leading institutions are too rigid to permit timely transformation. Social and cultural complexity coupled with a degenerating environment create unmanageable stresses; the social order is exposed to a series of crises. After a period of instability, uncertainty, and growing discontent, conflict degenerates into violence and the established order breaks down.

This could be the breakdown phase that begins in the second decade of the twenty-first century.

or

4 (b). The Breakthrough Scenario, 2010 and Beyond

The mindset of a critical mass of people evolves in time. The values and behaviors suggested by the new consciousness shift the dominant culture into a new and more adapted mode. As the new culture takes hold, an integrated world system emerges, capable of launching development aimed at ensuring access to the necessities of life for all people in every part of the world.

This is the positive development of our society that we can choose for our future.

A wise choice is vital, because if our Logos-dominated civilization fails to adapt to the conditions it has itself created, the entire economic and political structure of our world will come crashing down.

Let's review the developments that have brought us to the macroshift we face today.

THE BUILD-UP PERIOD OF 1860–1960

Until the second half of the eighteenth century, the eight thousand years that separated the Neolithic from the Industrial Age saw relatively few fundamental technological innovations. Basic agricultural tools were refined but not substantially modified: the sickle, the hoe, the chisel, the saw, the hammer, and the knife continued in use in substantially unchanged forms. More radical changes occurred only in regard to the technologies of irrigation and the introduction of new varieties of plants.

However, in the second half of the nineteenth century, led by the prior discovery of the power of steam, the Industrial Revolution brought an entire battery of new technologies on the scene. The first breakthroughs occurred in textiles: innovations in spinning cotton stimulated related inventions leading to machines capable of factory-based mass production. Industrial development soon spread from textiles to iron, as cheaper cast iron replaced more expensive wrought iron.

Closely following on the heels of innovations in the machine tool industry were developments in the chemical industry. Many of the twentieth-century technologies in the automobile, steel, cement, petrochemical, and pharmaceutical industries were spawned in the 1860s and the years that followed. Modern steel mills are for the most part still based on the Bessemer steel process developed at that time; the rotary kiln, patented by Fredrick Rancome in 1885, is still used in today's cement production; and the synthetic dyes of the late eighteenth century were basic to the development of modern chemical industries. The traction-based combustion engine, a key innovation in modern transportation, appeared in the 1880s simultaneously with Edison's electric light bulb and followed by Marconi's wireless and the Wright brothers' flying machine.

In the course of the twentieth century these technological innovations shifted industrial production from coal and steam, textiles,

machine tools, glass, pre-Bessemer forged steel, and labor intensive agriculture, to electricity, the internal combustion engine,
organic chemistry, and large-scale manufacturing.

THE GLOBALIZATION PERIOD, 1960 TO THE PRESENT

In the early 1960s, some one hundred years after the innovations
that led to the unfolding of the first industrial revolution, a new
type of technological innovation occurred. The "second industrial
revolution" replaced reliance on massive energy and raw material
inputs with the more intangible resource known as information. In
the last quarter of the twentieth century a rapidly growing quantity
of information came to be stored on optical disks, communicated by
fiber optics, with computers equipped with sophisticated programs
elaborating the data. The new "soft" technologies made the classical "hard" technologies more efficient but did not replace the materialistic purposes for which they were developed. Sophisticated
information technologies rationalized and dropped the cost of production and consumption and led to vast increments in the mining,
production, use, and ultimately discard of the manufactured goods
produced by hard technologies.

The spread of industrial technologies to the four corners of the
globe produced a series of profound transformations, globalizing
the economic and financial sectors while leaving social structures
locally diverse and disparate. For a minority it brought new wealth
and great increases in the material standard of living, but for the
growing masses it brought deepening poverty and seemingly hope-
less marginalization. Uneven and imbalanced globalization sparked
a new gold rush for the wealth promised by the high-technology
service and production sectors. The unreflective rush for wealth
broke apart traditional structures and placed in question established values and priorities. It led to the exploitation, and occa-
sionally overexploitation, of both renewable and nonrenewable
resources, and it degraded the livability of the urban as well as the
rural environment.

The Decisive Period, 2001–2010

By the end of the twentieth century globalization reached a new phase: the world system became increasingly and visibly unsustainable. This will have predictable consequences. By the end of the first decade of the twenty-first century society will enter the macroshift's chaos leap phase, triggered by high levels of stress, including conflict in the political sphere, vulnerability in the economic arena, volatility in the financial sphere, and worsening problems with climate and the environment. It will be only a matter of years before the progressive globalization of the economy coupled with intensifying contact among disparately developed cultures and societies reach a crucial decision point. If the processes initiated in the 1860s and accelerating since the 1960s continue without change, breakdown will follow.

Even if globalization in some sectors of the economy and the growth of interaction and interdependence among peoples and cultures are irreversible processes, the nature of the transformation they bring is not fated. In a chaotic system there are alternative evolutionary paths. In the early twenty-first century chaos can lead either to a sustainably balanced global world or to local and global crises and consequent breakdown. We will place our feet on the one path or the other by the way we internalize the emerging conditions in our priorities, values, and aspirations—that is, in our culture and our consciousness.

The Breakdown Period, 2010 and Beyond

Rigidity and lack of foresight will lead to stresses that the established institutions can no longer contain. Conflict erupts, and violence and anarchy follow in its wake.

or

The Breakthrough Period, 2010 and Beyond

A new way of thinking with more adapted values and more evolved consciousness will catalyze creativity in society. People and institutions learn to navigate the macroshift, mastering the stresses that arose in the wake of the previous generation's unreflective fascination with technology, wealth, and power. A new era dawns: the era of a sustainable post-Logos civilization.

3

Decisive Factors in Today's Macroshift

As WE ENTER THE THIRD MILLENNIUM the kinds of relations that have evolved between people, and between people and nature, create increased tensions, conflicts, and crises. Both sets of relations—the ecological as well as the social—are now unsustainable. To bring today's macroshift to a safe conclusion and pull ourselves up by our bootstraps to a more balanced post-Logos civilization, we must understand and reckon with these "unsustainabilities."

Ecological Unsustainabilities

Unsustainable relations have evolved on this planet between human societies and nature as a consequence of the unfolding of two basic trends:

- the rapid growth of demand by a growing population for the planet's physical and biological resources, and

- the accelerating depletion of many of the planet's physical and biological resources to satisfy these demands.

If these trends continue, the curves described by their unfolding will cross, and humanity's demand will exceed the planet's capacity for satisfying it. This will be an unprecedented situation.

For most of our five-million-year history, humanity's demand in relation to the available resources has been insignificant. With our primitive technologies and smaller numbers, planetary resources seemed limitless. Even when the technologies employed exhausted a local environment and depleted local resources, there were always other resources and environments to exploit. But by the middle of the nineteenth century the human population reached 1 billion, and it is more than 6 billion today. Our population is expected to be around 7.2 billion in 2015 and may grow to 8 billion or 10 billion by the middle of this century. Approximately 95 percent of this growth will occur in the presently poor countries and regions, but massive migrations will diffuse human populations to all the economically inhabitable areas of the globe.

Yet human numbers alone do not explain the current unsustainabilities. Today's 6 billion humans constitute only about 0.014 percent of the biomass of life on Earth, and 0.44 percent of the biomass of animals. Such a small fragment need not constitute a threat to the entire system, and hence itself. But because of excessive resource use and environmental degradation, we do threaten the entire system. Our impact on Earth's resources is entirely out of proportion to our size, and we cannot increase these demands indefinitely.

The current ecological unsustainabilities are the result of a mode of development that is as old as civilization. Prehistoric societies were stable and enduring: they evolved a sustainable relationship with their environment. Only the energy of the sun entered the nature–human system, and only the heat radiated into space left it—everything else was cycled and recycled within it. Food and water came from the local environment and were returned into that environment. Even in death the human body did not leave the ecological system: it entered the soil and contributed to its fertility. Nothing that men and women brought into being accumulated as "nonbiodegradable" toxins; nothing we did caused lasting damage to nature's cycles of generation and regeneration. The situation changed when groups of early humans learned to manipulate the environment and broke open the loop of regeneration that earlier tribes maintained. With this change, the human impact on the natural environment began its fateful increase.

> ∼ *Today we are operating at the outer edge of the planet's capacity to sustain human life. The Earth is a finite system, with finite space, resources, and regenerative potentials, and we are now exceeding the effective range of these limits.* ∼

As better tools and implements were invented, more resources could be accessed and existing resources could be better exploited. As a result, the population could, and did, grow. With the control of fire, perishable foods could be maintained over longer periods, and people gathered food and hunted over more extensive territories. Human settlements spread over the continents and began to transform nature to fit their needs. No longer content to gather and hunt their food, our ancestors learned to plant seeds and use rivers for irrigation and the removal of wastes. They domesticated some species of dogs, horses, and cattle. These practices enabled our forebears to extend their dominion over vaster territories, but they also increased humanity's impact on nature. Nourishment began to flow from a purposively modified environment, and the growing wastes from larger and technologically more sophisticated communities continued to disappear conveniently, with smoke vanishing into thin air and solid waste washing downstream in rivers and dispersing in the seas. If a local environment gradually became arid and inhospitable—due to deforestation and overworking the soil—there was always virgin land to conquer and to exploit.

This is no longer the case today. We are operating at the outer edge of the planet's capacity to sustain human life. The Earth is a finite system, with finite space, resources, and regenerative potentials, and we are now exceeding the effective range of these limits.

Quantitative indices and measurements have been developed to calculate the level of human impact on nature. One such index is the ecological footprint: the area of land required to support a human community. If the footprint of a settlement is larger than the area of that settlement, the settlement is not independently sustainable. A city is intrinsically unsustainable, for example, because few of the natural resources used by its inhabitants come from within its borders; most come from hinterlands and catchments in regard to food, water, and other resources, and the disposal of wastes. But entire regions and countries could well be sustainable if their ecological footprint did not extend beyond their boundaries.

In a recent survey commissioned by the Earth Council of Costa Rica, the ecological footprints of fifty-two countries were examined. Forty-two of those countries had footprints that exceeded their territory. If other countries within the region had surplus ecological resources, this would still not spell global unsustainability, but this is not the case. The optimum sustainable resource level—where the current loss of topsoil is reduced and ultimately halted—is 1.7 hectares (one hectare is 10,000 square meters, or 2.471 acres). But the average per capita footprint of the countries examined came to 2.8 hectares. If this average load were reached by the more than 180 countries of the world, the ecological footprint of the human population would be larger than the whole of the biosphere. The only reason this is not the case today is because people in the poor countries have footprints of far less than 1.7 hectares. The extremes range from half a hectare in Bangladesh to 10.3 hectares in the United States.

The unsustainability of our load on nature is aggravated by the progressive impairment of the biosphere, which was not widely recognized until the 1980s. The evident success of technological civilization has obscured the fact that its life-supporting environment is becoming increasingly degraded. Chemically bolstered mechanized agriculture increases yields per acre and makes more acres available for cultivation, but it also increases the growth of algae that chokes lakes and waterways. Chemicals such as DDT are effective insecticides, but they poison entire animal, bird, and insect populations.

Waste disposal contributes to the nature-impairment process. Today we discard much more than our household wastes into the

environment. We also inject an estimated 100,000 chemical com-
pounds into the land, rivers, and seas; dump millions of tons of
sludge and solid waste into the oceans; release billions of tons of
CO_2 into the air; and increase the level of radioactivity in water,
land, air. The wastes discarded into the environment do not vanish;
they come back to plague those who produce them as well as other
communities near and far. Refuse dumped into the sea returns to
poison marine life and infest coastal regions. The smoke rising from
homesteads and factories does not dissolve and disappear: the CO_2
released remains in the atmosphere, affecting the world's weather.
In the rich countries some one million chemicals produced by
industry are bubbling through the groundwater systems; in poor
countries rivers and lakes have up to a hundred times the accepted
level of pollutants. Until recently, the water in Malaysia's Kelang
River had enough mercury to function as a pesticide.

Not surprisingly, there has been a massive increase in allergies in
both urban and rural populations. The appellations of toxic environmental effects constitute a whole new vocabulary: there is MCS
(multiple chemical sensitivity), wood preservative syndrome, sol-
vent intolerance, chemically associated immune dysfunction, clin-
ical ecology syndrome, chronic fatigue syndrome, fibromyalgia, and
sick building syndrome, among others.

Robert Muller, who spent more than forty years at the helm in the
United Nations and remained an inveterate optimist about the
future, was also a realist: as his comments to this report shows, he
recognized the urgent need for change. His data indicate that the
human impairment of nature proceeds at a completely unsustainable pace. Each *minute* 21 hectares (52 acres) of tropical forest are
lost, 50 tons of fertile topsoil are blown off, and 12,000 tons of carbon dioxide are added to the atmosphere (mainly as 35,725 barrels
of oil are burned as industrial and commercial fuel). Each *hour* 685
hectares (1,696 acres) of productive dryland become desert, and each
day 250,000 tons of sulfuric acid fall as acid rain in the northern
hemisphere. The degradation of water, air, and soil—three of the
most essential resources of nature—is especially threatening.

LANDMARKS IN THE DEGRADATION OF WATER, AIR, AND SOIL

Water, air, and soil are both overused and misused, and can no longer regenerate sufficiently to meet the demands of a growing population. Statistics from UNESCO, the Food and Agricultural Organization, and other U.N. and world bodies show us the details with striking clarity.

WATER

Four-fifths of the planet's surface is water, and the idea that humanity could run out of water seems preposterous. But water for human use has to be fresh, and the salt water in the oceans and seas makes up 97.5 percent of the planet's total water volume. Two-thirds of the remaining water is concentrated in polar icecaps and underground. The renewable fresh water potentially available for human consumption—water in lakes, rivers, and reservoirs—is no more than 0.007 percent of the water on the surface of the Earth. This relatively thin trickle is essential, however: one can survive for about a month without food but no more than a week without water.

In the past the available water reserves were more than enough to satisfy human needs. Even in 1950, there was a potential world reserve of nearly 17,000 m^3 of fresh water for every woman, man, and child. However, the rate of water withdrawal has been more than double the rate of population growth, and in 1999 this reserve amount decreased to 7,300 m^3. If current trends continue, in the year 2025 there will be only 4,800 m^3 of reserves per person. This would create serious water shortages in many parts of the world.

Just fifty years ago there was not a country in the world that would have faced catastrophic water shortages. Today about one-third of the world's population lives under nearly catastrophic conditions, and by 2025 two-thirds of the population will have to cope with such conditions. Europe and the United States will have half the per capita reserves they had in 1950, and Asia and Latin America will have but a quarter. The worst hit countries will be in Africa, the Middle East, and south and central Asia. Here the available supplies may drop to less than 1,700 m^3 per person.

The World Health Organization, the World Meteorological Organization, the U.N. Environment Programme, and UNESCO foresee serious local and regional water emergencies by around 2005. By 2025 the descending supply curve will intersect the ascending demand curve. This will create unlivable conditions for nearly five billion people—two-thirds of the then-living population—and it will also create serious social and political conflicts, migrations, epidemics, and worsening environmental degradation.

AIR

The further idea, that we could overexploit the atmosphere that surrounds the planet, seems just as unlikely. After all, this is an envelope some twenty kilometers deep, spread evenly from the polar icecaps to the tropical equator. The amount of air that humans, or even all living organisms taken together, need is minuscule compared to this vast supply. But just as with water, it is not a question of how much we need, but in what form we need it. It is a question of quality rather than quantity. Salty or polluted water is not of much use when it comes to ensuring the survival of the human population, and polluted air of poor quality is also of little use. Yet we are changing the composition of the planet's atmosphere without regard to its impact. We are reducing the atmosphere's oxygen content and increasing its carbon dioxide (as well as other greenhouse gas) content. These are unsustainable trends.

Evidence from prehistoric times indicates an oxygen content above today's 21 percent of total volume. Oxygen in the air has decreased in recent times mainly due to the burning of coal, which began in the middle of the nineteenth century. The current oxygen content of the Earth's atmosphere dips to 19 percent over impacted areas and is down to 12 to 17 percent over the major cities. These provide insufficient oxygen to keep body cells and organs, and the entire immune system, functioning at full efficiency. At the levels reached today, cancers and other degenerative diseases are likely to develop, and at levels of 6 to 7 percent, life can no longer be sustained.

Our impact on the atmosphere has resulted in a reduction in oxygen, but it has produced an increase in some other elements. The increase in atmospheric greenhouse gases is particularly significant. During the current interglacial period—a period that has already lasted some 11,000 to 12,000 years—the chemical composition of the atmosphere has been relatively stable, with about 280 parts of carbon dioxide per million. Two hundred years of burning fossil fuels and cutting

down large tracts of forest have increased the atmosphere's carbon dioxide content. Currently CO_2 exceeds 350 parts per million and is growing rapidly. Gases
released by the use of aerosols and refrigerants have produced a related problem: they have seriously depleted the atmosphere's ozone layer. The well-publi-
cized "ozone hole" over the Antarctic has been spreading, increasing the
incidence of skin cancer in numerous countries.

The continuing emission of greenhouse gases is a threat both to bodily health
and to the global food supply. Recent surveys indicate that more than 80 percent of some 105 European cities exceed World Health Organization (WHO) air
quality standards for at least one pollutant. Elsewhere the situation is still worse.
Pollutant levels in Beijing, Delhi, Jakarta, and Mexico City exceed WHO standards
by a factor of three or more, and in some cities in China particulate levels exceed
them by a factor of six.

Global food supply is affected as changes in the chemical composition of the
atmosphere trigger a change in the climate. An atmosphere with a high composition of CO_2 and other man-made gases traps heat from the sun, creates a
greenhouse effect, warms up the atmosphere and changes the weather. Temperatures in the Western Arctic are currently at a four-hundred-year high. Since
1940, average temperatures in the Arctic region have risen by 2.5°C and some
42 percent of the icecap has already melted. Because the temperature of the Arctic Ocean is rising, the ice is breaking up earlier than usual and huge icebergs
are threatening fishing vessels in the area. With a further increase in global
warming the volume of fresh water streaming into the North Atlantic would bring
along enough icebergs to deflect the Gulf Stream. That would flood Western
Europe with frigid waters, creating winters of Siberian cold over much of the
continent. While Europe is threatened with a colder climate, most of the planet
is subjected to rising temperatures. From 1975 to 1999 the average temperature
of the Earth increased from 13.94°C to 14.35°C. All of the warmest twenty-three
years since record keeping began in 1866 have occurred since 1975.

Global warming interferes with agricultural production: in cold regions with short
growing seasons it could increase yields, but it is likely to decrease harvests in
tropical and subtropical areas where crops are already growing near the limit of
their heat tolerance. These effects are not precisely foreseeable—global warming is not a gradual and distributed process but a differential warming and cool-
ing effect over different parts of the globe. It is accompanied by extreme and

violent weather patterns. The occurrence of hurricanes over tropical areas will be intensified, together with massive downpours in temperate zones.

As polar ice melts, sea level will rise, possibly by as much as 21 centimeters by the year 2050. This will be a threat to nearly 80 million people living in coastal regions at or below the current sea level. Rising sea levels would create millions of refugees in China, India, Indonesia, Vietnam, Bangladesh, and the Philippines, migrating inland and exacerbating conditions in already overcrowded interiors.

Global warming is having an impact on our health. Violent storms, floods, and droughts threaten life; illnesses and deaths increase during heat waves, especially in urban areas and among the infirm and the elderly. With weather changes, infectious diseases such as malaria and dengue fever, which are carried by mosquitoes, can spread, and higher sea levels and periodic floodings create additional pressure on the supply of safe drinking water.

TOPSOIL

With the exception of sandy deserts and high mountains, the surface of the continents is covered with soil, but soil of a quality suitable for agriculture is relatively scarce. The U.N.'s Food and Agriculture Organization estimates that there are 3,031 million hectares (about 7,490 million acres) of high-quality cropland currently available, 71 percent of which is in the developing world. This is a precious resource, desperately needed to supply the food and agricultural needs of a growing human population. Yet pressures of human activity produce erosion, destructuring, compaction, impoverishment, excessive desiccation, accumulation of toxic salts, leaching of nutritious elements, and urban and industrial pollution. Lands degraded to desert-like conditions reduce the world's food and agricultural production for centuries; it takes nature one hundred to four hundred years to create 10 millimeters of productive topsoil. To build a topsoil layer of 30 centimeters takes anywhere from three thousand to twelve thousand years.

For the past few decades we have lost 5 to 7 million hectares (12 to 17 million acres) of cropland per year. If this process continues, some 30 million hectares will be lost by mid-century, leaving 2.7 billion hectares (about 6.67 billion acres) to support 8 to 10 billion people. This would yield an average of 0.3 hectares (or 0.74 acres) per person—the bare subsistence level of food production for the entire human population.

Social Unsustainabilities

The unsustainability of relations between humans and nature is aggravated by growing tension within and among humans. Social relations are becoming just as unsustainable as life-supporting conditions in the environment.

> *Globalization proceeds at a breakneck pace, but many countries and population segments are left out of it. . . . The world is growing together in some respects and is coming apart in others.*

Economic growth still occurs, and is likely to continue, but it is not a panacea. The globalization of the economy is highly uneven. It is driven by the search for higher material living standards and promoted by the spread of information technologies and the increasing dynamism of the private sector. In the areas of information, communication, trade, financial markets, and technologies, globalization proceeds at a breakneck pace, but many countries and population segments are left out of it. These countries face social upheaval and political instability as their have-not population increases. The world is growing together in some respects and is coming apart in others. The richest 20 percent earn 90 times the income of the poorest 20 percent, consume 11 times as much energy, eat 11 times as much meat, have 49 times the number of telephones, and own 145 times the number of cars. The net worth of the more than 500 billionaires of this world (of which about a third come from the developing countries) is roughly $1,110 billion—equal to the net worth of half the world population.

The rich-poor gap is a major cause of social unsustainability in the contemporary world. If access to the planet's physical and biological resources were evenly distributed, the situation would be less critical. If food supplies, for example, were equally shared, every person would receive about a hundred calories more than are required to replace the 1,800 to 3,000 calories he or she expends each day (the average healthy diet calls for about 2,600 calories). But people in the rich countries of North America, Western Europe, and Japan obtain 140 percent of the caloric requirements of normal health, whereas people in the poorest countries, such as Madagascar, Guyana and Laos, are limited to 70 percent. Americans spend only 10 percent of their income on food—and still buy so much that they throw away 15 percent of it. Haitians, some 600 miles to the south, as well as three-fourths of all Africans, spend more than half their income on food and are undernourished. Surveys by the U.N. Development Programme and the Food and Agriculture Organization indicate that eighty-seven countries today can neither produce sufficient food to sustain their population nor have the money to import the missing amount from elsewhere.

The world's pattern of energy consumption is just as disparate. Even if there are great disparities in living standards between the industrialized North and the mainly rural South, the averages speak volumes. The average of the few well-off and the many poor Africans, for example, is half a kilowatt hour of commercial electrical energy per person. The corresponding average for Asians and Latin Americans is 2–3 kWh, and Americans, Europeans, Australians and Japanese use up to 8 kWh each. With 4.1 percent of the world population, the United States alone consumes 25 percent of the world's energy production, much of it wastefully—for example, by heating homes with inefficient gas-powered heaters or electric radiators in the winter, leaving air conditioners on for extended periods in the summer, and using gas-guzzling vans, pick-up trucks, and sport utility vehicles for everyday transportation. The average American burns 5 tons of fossil fuel per year—in contrast with the 0.8 tons of the average Chinese and the relatively modest 2.9 tons of the average German. It is estimated that in the 80-plus years of the expected life span of a child born to a middle-class family in the United States, he or she will consume 800,000 kilowatts of electrical energy. In addition, he or she will also consume 2,500,000 liters of water; 21,000 tons of gasoline; 220,000 kilos of steel; the wood of 1,000 trees, and will generate 60 tons of municipal waste. At these rates the average American child will produce twice the environmental load of a Swedish child, 3 times that of an Italian, 13 times that of a Brazilian, 35 times that of an Indian, and 280 times that of a Haitian.

Affluent consumption is not the only cause of the unsustainability of the modern world; the way poor people attempt to obtain the resources required for their survival is a problem as well. The 1.3 billion people who, according to World Bank estimates, live at or below the absolute poverty line (defined as the equivalent of one dollar a day or less), destroy the environment on which they depend. In many areas of Africa, central Asia, and the Indian subcontinent, women and children spend on average four to six hours searching for fuel wood and as long drawing and carrying water. With rural environments degrading, people abandon their native towns and villages and flee to the cities. Urban complexes have experienced explosive growth: one out of every three people now lives in a city, and by the year 2025 two out of every three are expected to do so. By that year there will be more than five hundred cities with populations of over one million, and thirty megacities exceeding eight million. Such cities are intrinsically unsustainable. The bigger they are, the greater their dependence on the already overexploited countryside.

Sociocultural stresses threaten the stability of life in today's societies. Traditional social structures are breaking down: the family is a prime example. In many parts of the world the family, sociologists say, has become "defunctionalized." That is, the functions of family life have been taken over by institutions dominated by outside interest groups. Child rearing is increasingly entrusted to kindergartens and company or community daycare centers. Leisure-time activities are dominated by the marketing and PR efforts of commercial enterprises, and the provision of daily nourishment is shifting from the family kitchen to supermarkets, prepared food industries, and fast-food chains. In many developing countries the state's promotion of family planning technologies colors the most intimate husband-wife relations.

In cities the exigencies of economic survival and an insistence on modern lifestyles eliminate the traditional extended family, and extreme poverty breaks apart the nuclear family itself. To make ends meet, women and children must often work, and women are extensively exploited, being offered menial jobs for low pay. Children fare even worse. According to the International Labour Office, 50 million children are working in the world today, for the most part in Africa, Asia, and Latin America. They are employed for a pittance in factories, mines, and on the land, and many others are forced to venture into the hazards of life on the street as "self-employed" vendors or just plain beggars.

An even more deplorable consequence of family poverty is the letting-go, and sometimes the outright selling, of children into prostitution. UNICEF names this "one of the most abusive, exploitative and hazardous forms of child labour." In Asia alone, one million children are believed to work as juvenile prostitutes, exploited by the highly profitable and growing industries of international pedophilia, fueled by widespread sex tourism.

Whether in the cities or in the countryside, poverty is characterized by malnutrition, joblessness, and unjust and degrading conditions of life. At the same time it makes for the overworking of productive lands, the contamination of rivers and lakes, and the lowering of water tables. This creates a vicious cycle. Poverty encourages high birthrates, because children help subsistence families garner the resources needed for survival. Population growth creates more poverty, and more poor people destroy more of the environment while rending the functional structures on which social stability vitally depends.

CHINA: A SOCIOECOLOGICAL CATASTROPHE IN THE MAKING

In China social and ecological unsustainability is more critical than in most other countries of the world. Though it is generally thought that China is only now moving into the Industrial Age, it is actually moving out of it—into an uncertain future.

Modern China has a checkered past to look back on, and an uncertain future to look forward to. Under Chairman Mao a supposedly enlightened dictatorship became repressive and inhumane. In the post-Mao era a more enlightened but hardly less hierarchical structure has been created to bring China into the global world of production and competition. It has made fabulous progress, but whether its success will be enduring will depend not on what its leadership wants but on what it refuses to face: the country's fundamental socioecological unsustainability.

Currently China's population is five times that of the United States, while its cultivated land is one-tenth as much. As a result, China is feeding 22 percent of the world's population on 7 percent of the world's agricultural land, with 7 percent of the world's fresh water reserves. For now China manages this feat by employing an enormous agricultural labor force, estimated at 40 percent of the world total, and by pumping vast quantities of chemical fertilizers and other chemicals into the soil. The result is a high level of soil rigidity and aridity. Of her 100 million hectares of cultivated land, one-tenth is already highly polluted; one-third is suffering from water loss and soil erosion; one-fifteenth is salinized, and nearly 4 percent is in the process of turning into a desert. Due to urban sprawl and building roads and factories in the three decades from the mid-1950s to the mid-1980s, 15 million hectares of cultivated land were turned to nonagricultural use—an area equal to the agricultural lands of France and Italy combined. The remaining lands face a productivity crisis. The shortfall in grain, for example, is expected to reach 10 percent of the country's requirement within the next few years.

Nearly half of China's industrial output is generated by village enterprises, which require high inputs, have low productivity, and produce high levels of pollution. The biggest pollutants are the small paper mills. Though the government ordered the most dangerous ones closed, the majority refused, and only 3 percent of those that refused were forced to shut down. The industrial pollution problem is aggravated by the country's dominant mode of energy production: 75 percent is based on burning coal. As a result, 40 percent of the country's total land area is subject to acid rain. Another cause of pollution is the rapid increase in the population of cars: the air over 99 percent of the 600 major cities is below internationally recognized air quality standards. Some 85 percent of the industrial wastewater and 90 percent of the urban effluents are discharged into rivers, lakes, and the sea without treatment. More than four-fifth of the 191 tributaries of the Huaihe River, for example, are blackish-green. Some 80 percent of the rivers and 45 percent of the underground water tables have been polluted, and 76 percent of the drinking water fails minimal health standards. Half the waste treatment equipment acquired as part of the 23.4 billion yuan of investment in preventing and controlling pollution in the 1980s is either not in regular operation or has been abandoned altogether. Urban and industrial refuse remain unsorted in open garbage heaps that choke the principal cities.

China's unsustainability is a consequence of the current condition of her cities and countryside, an annual loss of 700,000 hectares of land, and an annual population increase of fourteen million. A country of more than 1.2 billion people facing urban health problems and diminishing agricultural yields makes for a catastrophe that is of local origin but is likely to have a global impact.

Sufficient investment in the resources and the infrastructures people and economies truly need could remedy the vicious cycle of poverty breeding more poverty; there is enough money in the world economy to help the poor countries overcome the worst aspects of deprivation and penury. The $214 billion owed by the most indebted developing countries is equivalent to just 4.5 months of Western military spending. Some $19 trillion is currently invested in the world's stock markets alone—the equivalent of the combined gross domestic product of the G-8 industrialized countries, and nearly 80 percent of the whole world's GDP. Where this money goes has an enormous impact on the direction taken by the global economy, putting unparalleled power in the hands of international investors to influence the state of the world. More than two-thirds of direct foreign investment goes to the richest 20 percent of the population; only 1 percent reaches the poorest 20 percent.

The financial community operates on the classical assumption that "the market ensures optimal capital allocation through the efficient incorporation of all available and relevant information into share prices." This is true provided that the available information includes *all* the relevant items. This, unfortunately, is not the case.

Global corporations, the major sources of investment-related information, do not consider sustainability issues relevant to investment analysis and decision making, and they seldom provide information on the sustainability of the practices and projects they fund by external investments. Independent investment professionals could fill this gap, yet the typical professional lacks the competence to assess issues of ecological and social sustainability. Most of those who do have such competence work for international organizations and public-benefit social and environmental institutions. Their reports, though well-meaning and relevant, are aimed at the general public and usually are not standardized, are inconsistent, and sometimes are unverified. As such they are of little use to investors who categorize them as stating an emotional issue that is irrelevant to day-to-day investment decisions.

One cannot globalize one sector of the world and rend another. The new technologies of information and communication drive toward a global world, but the institutions and mechanisms responsible for managing the globalizing process lag behind.

The bottom line is that the world today is both ecologically and socially unsustainable. This situation cannot be prolonged indefinitely. One cannot globalize one sector of the world and rend another. The new technologies of information and communication drive toward a global world, but the institutions and mechanisms responsible for managing the globalizing process lag behind.

It is time to recognize that the macroshift we are living through has brought profound change. Its processes of rapid but one-sided globalization have led to a chaotic period. The outcome is undetermined, but the basic alternatives are evident. They are either breakdown in conflict and crisis, or breakthrough to a new civilization. The choice is in our hands.

4

The Choice

THE TRANSFORMATION WROUGHT BY A MACROSHIFT has always
challenged the creativity of people, but today's challenge is
unprecedented. In the past, a more adapted civilization evolved over
several generations; the rhythm of change was relatively slow. This
is no longer the case. The critical period for change today is compressed within the lifetime of a single generation. Repeated trial
and error may have sufficed in the past, but it is not adequate today.
The overexploitation of resources and impairment of nature, coupled with the unequal distribution of wealth and the destruction of
the fabric of societies, has launched us on an irreversible transformation. In a macroshift many things are possible, but remaining
with the status quo is not among them. We can neither go backward
nor stay put; we can only go forward. But the direction of change
is not predetermined; we have a choice.

*⁓ A Chinese proverb warns, "If we do not change direction, we
are likely to end up exactly where we are headed." ⁓*

But just what is this choice—and who will make it? A Chinese
proverb warns, "If we do not change direction, we are likely to end
up exactly where we are headed." Applied to contemporary humanity, this would be disastrous. Without a change in direction we are

on the way to a world of increasing population pressure and spreading poverty; growing social and political conflict potential; accelerating climate change and food and energy shortages; worsening industrial, urban, and agricultural pollution of air, water, and soil; further destruction of the ozone layer; accelerating reduction of biodiversity; and continued loss of atmospheric oxygen. We also run the risk of megadisasters caused by nuclear accidents and leaking nuclear waste, devastating floods and tornadoes due to climate change, and widespread health problems due to toxic additives in food and drink and the accumulation of toxins in soil, air, and water.

These risks are real, since the great bulk of humanity in societies both rich and poor, Western and traditional, remains fascinated by material goods, personal wealth, and ostentatious lifestyles. Many people hold a mechanistic view of nature: we are free to manipulate the environment as we wish without regard for the consequences. Many also hold a Darwinistic view of society: life is a struggle for survival, with the powerful reaping rightful rewards and accumulating wealth that the market will hopefully distribute. The universe at large is a passive backdrop to human actions, governed by science's deterministic laws, if not by divine fiat. In any case, individual actions have hardly any impact on the wider environment. In consequence people feel no responsibility for what happens in and to the world around them. In the end, a breakdown becomes inevitable.

THE BREAKDOWN SCENARIO

The persistent pursuit of material goods and grandiose lifestyles overexploits resources and impoverishes the environment. As unfavorable weather patterns limit harvests and yields are further reduced by a shortage of unpolluted water, hunger and disease spread among the two billion poorest of the poor. Mass migrations get under way, as people move from the hardest hit areas to areas still relatively well off. Governments find themselves under mounting pressure; one after the other resort to military measures to shore up crumbling borders, ensure access to basic resources for their people, and "cleanse" their territories of unwanted populations.

A rise in military expenditures diverts money from health and environmental care, aggravating the plight of poor populations and worsening the condition of the environment. This results in lower yields, greater deprivation, and more conflict potentials, increasing the need for military measures in a vicious cycle that feeds on itself.

A constant series of emergencies concentrates power in the hands of national politicians and military juntas, and cyberspace is dominated by the shrinking minority that has the means to promote its own interests. The Internet itself resembles a giant shopping mall and a forum for special interest groups. It encourages consumerism and reinforces the belief that the true aim of life is to make money and lead a carefree and unconstrained existence.

The international community becomes increasingly polarized, with growing gaps and resentment between those who benefit from globalization of the world's economic, financial, and information systems, and those who are locked out of it. Marginalized states, ethnic groups, and organizations become more and more frustrated. They take advantage of the high-speed information environment to make contact with each other and begin to cooperate. Strategic alliances hostile to globalization and the power of major states and global enterprises are formed.

Terrorist groups, nuclear proliferators, narcotraffickers, and organized crime find a fertile environment for pursuing their goals. They form alliances with unscrupulous entrepreneurs and expand the scale and scope of their activities, corrupting leaders in the marginalized states, infiltrating troubled banks and businesses, and cooperating with insurgents to control more and more territory. Traffic in narcotics, in alien smuggling, in women and children, as well as in hazardous wastes and toxic materials joins traffic in illicit biological, chemical, and nuclear weapons and becomes a global enterprise.

In this disordered world, international cooperation is more and more difficult, and finally impossible. As crisis follows crisis, humanity faces the prospect of a worldwide breakdown.

A global breakdown is just one of the possible outcomes of the macroshift we are experiencing today. There is a brighter prospect, illustrated by the "breakthrough scenario." In this scenario we wake up to the need to transform our thinking and behavior to cope with the dangers we face. A new sense of urgency to live and act effectively and responsibly is joined with a renewed sense of commitment to each other and the common future. We begin to recognize that we are a vital link in a network of great complexity that is highly sensitive to human values and actions. We develop a sense of individual empowerment and a deeper spirituality, which enable us to see the planet as a living organism and ourselves as conscious elements of it.

THE BREAKTHROUGH SCENARIO

The need to live and act in ways suited to life for six billion in an already impaired environment triggers advocacy of a new behavioral code. "Let's try to live in a way that enables others to live as well" is beginning to take precedence over the time-honored "live and let live (as long as it doesn't interfere with me)" by the well-off and "let me live like the rich" by the poor. A new vision of self, others, and nature surfaces on the Internet, on television, and in the communication networks of enterprises, communities, and ethnic groups. Global businesses are sensitized to the changing values of their clients and customers and respond with goods and services that meet this shift in demand. Global news and entertainment media explore fresh perspectives and emerging social and cultural innovations. The public's goals and ambitions become reoriented—toward "the good life" conceived not as amassing the greatest possible amount of money and material goods but as finding meaningful personal relationships and caring for others and for nature.

Population pressures combined with resource shortages encourage people to pull together rather than to pull apart. There is growing public support for public policies and corporate strategies that manifest a higher level of social and ecological responsibility. Funds and capital are channeled from military and defense applications and the demands of the affluent minority to the needs of the people who make up the bulk of society. Measures are implemented to safeguard the environment, create an effective system of food and resource distribution, and develop and put to work sustainable energy, transport, and agricultural technologies. More and more people have access to food, jobs, and education. More and more people enter the Internet and other communication systems as active dialogue partners. Their communication reinforces solidarity and uncovers further areas of mutual interest.

By the second decade of the twenty-first century the world community is ready to put into place a series of system-building measures combined with sweeping system reforms. When the new arrangements take shape, national, international and intercultural mistrust, ethnic conflict, racial oppression, economic inequity, and gender inequality begin to give way to mutual trust and respect and a readiness to form partnerships and cooperate. Insistence on self-sufficiency and autonomy are joined with shared concern for nature and for others. Rather than breaking down in conflicts and wars, the human family is on the way to breaking through to a sustainable world of interlinked yet self-reliant communities.

The choice between these two scenarios—and others less radical but not altogether different from them—is in our hands. This choice does not lie with big business and big government but with ordinary people. It is up to you and me to choose a sustainable civilization that harmonizes the diversity of the world with the globalization of its technologies and markets and the interaction and interdependence of its economies.

> ∿ *The crucial issue is not* how many *people use the planet's* resources but *how* they use them. *Our world has enough, as Gandhi said, to provide for people's* need, *but not enough to provide for their* greed. ∿

Creating a sustainable civilization calls for an ongoing dynamic balance between human needs and demands and adequate access to basic resources. If the human population keeps growing, and if its patterns of production and consumption remain as disparate as they are today, achieving this balance will not be possible. Even though economic growth will continue and the demographic curve will slacken, by the middle of the twenty-first century some 90 percent of the world's population will live in today's poor regions. Fortunately, the crucial issue is not *how many* people use the planet's resources but *how* they use them. Our world has enough, as Gandhi said, to provide for people's *need*, but not enough to provide for their *greed*.

In the industrialized parts of the world greed is now dominant. In the name of freedom and laissez-faire capitalism, obsolete values and beliefs give free reign to selfishness and ostentation. People seldom admit such traits even to themselves, but it is evident in many aspects of everyday behavior. One man in a small town in the Sonoran Desert of Arizona decided to admit this not just to himself but to everyone. In December of 2000 in a letter to the local newspaper he listed 39 items that he said makes him a "Bad American." Among other things he wrote: "I don't care about appearing compassionate"; "I think I am better than homeless bums"; "I paid for it and I don't care to recycle it. You may do so if you please"; "I think global warming is bullshit!"; and "I like big cars, and big houses, and golf at my private club."

Living by such values and aspirations entails excessive consumption and excessive waste. Those who "enjoy" such a living standard use 80 percent of the world's energy and raw materials and contribute the lion's share of its pollution. For example, the average person needs 5 liters of water a day for drinking and cooking and 25 liters for personal hygiene. But the average American uses 350 liters a day—80 liters just for flushing the toilet—and the average European and Japanese 165 liters. At the same time, many Africans walk 2 miles to get safe water, if indeed they can get any, and 48 percent of them lack access to water that is safe for drinking and cooking.

Selfishness and greed also affect the way people eat. Affluent people consume vast quantities of red meat and bottled drinks. The world's entire grain harvest would not be enough to feed all the cattle needed if everyone worldwide were to adopt these dietary habits. The average Englishman consumes six bags of chips, six chocolate bars, six bags of candy, three sandwiches, two pies, two burgers, a donut, and a kebab every month while sitting behind the wheel. And each year Americans, worried about obesity, spend 30 times more trying to slim down than the annual U.N. budget for famine relief.

Affluent people overuse the planet's resources, and poor people misuse them. Of the six billion people on the planet, the two billion rich and "developed" consume and waste more than their share, while the two billion poor and "underdeveloped" misuse what little is left to them. To make things worse, many of the two billion in the middle who belong to the emancipating and thus "developing" masses hope to adopt the lifeways and consumption patterns of the two billion "developed." But this ambition is more than the resources and ecosystems of the planet can fulfill.

> ∼ *The life ways and consumption patterns of the rich are stressful and unhealthy and can lead to hypertension, stroke, heart disease, and cancer. The very ideal of material luxury is flawed. . . . Clearly, there are more satisfying ways to live the good life.* ∼

Not only do the rich need to adopt better ways, the poor need to adopt better aspirations. When poor people believe that by emulating the ways of the rich they improve the quality of their lives, they are sadly mistaken. A high material standard of living does not automatically mean a high quality of life. The life ways and consumption patterns of the rich are stressful and unhealthy and can lead to hypertension, stroke, heart disease, and cancer. The very ideal of material luxury is flawed. Take the height of luxury offered by the popular tourist industry: sitting in the sun, smoking a cigarette, sipping a daiquiri, munching on a hamburger, and talking on the cellular phone. One who lives up to this ideal increases his or her chances of getting skin cancer, lung cancer, cirrhosis of the liver, high cholesterol, and brain damage. This is not much of an improvement over staying at home and working in a high-pressure job, taking smoke breaks every hour, drinking a martini after work to relax, and going to sleep in front of the television.

Clearly, there are more satisfying ways to live the good life. There are meaningful and important tasks to be achieved in every job and profession, and there are scores of healthy and rewarding ways to spend leisure time. Helping neighbors, creating a better community, visiting sites of natural, historical, or cultural interest, hiking, swimming, biking, reading, listening to music, or taking an interest in literature and culture are all satisfying pursuits that do not involve a high level of material and energy consumption and do not require a lot of money. Yet they are healthier for us and better for our soul, and easier on the environment than the current models for success, affluence, and luxury.

> ◯ *If mad cow disease results in weaning people from a red-meat diet, in the long term this may be not a bane but a blessing. Eating fresh produce, living closer to nature, and walking more and using public transportation are healthier than eating red meat and junk food, sitting in cars in overcrowded streets and arteries, and breathing polluted air.* ◯

Nevertheless, the lifestyles of the affluent are widely admired and emulated. Because the two billion "developed" drive a private car to work, shopping, and recreation—even when public transport is available—the two billion "developing" hope to own and use cars for much the same reasons and the same purposes. A good portion of the 1.3 billion Chinese are on the way to realizing this ambition. In the center of the "miracle city" Shenzhen in the south there are hardly any bicycles left, but private cars, including luxury models, abound—together with traffic jams and air pollution. In India the "apartment culture" has become widespread; having a "luxury apartment" is considered the height of living the good life. Much the same emulation occurs in regard to eating habits. Because people in the industrialized countries have a preference for steaks and hamburgers, people in the developing countries aspire to the same kind of diet. Hamburger stands and fast-food restaurants are springing up throughout the poor countries and regions of the globe.

Suppose, then, that the two billion "developed" decided to live in a more responsible way. Would that make a difference to the aspirations of the two billion ambitiously "developing"—and the state of the two billion hopelessly "underdeveloped"? It very likely would. Though governments of industrialized countries tend to ignore it, simpler lifestyles and more responsible choices would free a significant portion of the planet's resources for consumption by all the people who inhabit it. For example, it takes the produce of 190 square meters of land and 105,000 liters of water to produce one kilogram of grain-fed feedlot beef. But to produce one kilogram of soybeans takes only 16 square meters of land and 9,000 liters of water. On the same amount of land where farmers catering to the preferences of the affluent now produce one kilogram of beef, they could produce nearly 12 kilograms of soybeans, or 8.6 kilograms of corn. And they would save 96,000 liters of water by choosing soybeans, and 92,500 liters by planting corn. Given the rapid erosion of many agricultural lands and the coming water squeeze, this difference may be crucial. If mad cow disease results in weaning people from a red-meat diet, in the long term this may be not a bane but a blessing. Eating fresh produce, living closer to nature, and walking more and using public transportation are healthier than eating red meat and junk food, sitting in cars in overcrowded streets and arteries, and breathing polluted air.

"Live more simply, so others can simply live," said Gandhi. Following this advice is even more urgent today than it was in his day. It is also easier to do. Today we realize that living simply is not a come-down. On the contrary, simple living is the fruit of a free choice that makes for greater personal well-being and a deeper sense of meaning in life. It is living in a way that is socially and ecologically sustainable and thus responsible to all the world's people, today and for generations to come.

There is no single solution to such a complex problem, and to achieve a better distribution of the world's basic resources our economic systems must be reformed. Yet such reform is unlikely without a shift in the values and preferences of a critical mass of society. Timely shifts in consumer preferences and civic and environmental aspirations would buy time for economic and political reform to be put in place and would help safeguard the environment, defusing the potential for conflict inherent in today's inequitable situation. When all is said and done, the critical factor in choosing our future is the choice we ourselves make about the way we consume, the way we work, and the way we live.

> We are the music makers,
> and we are the dreamers of dreams,
> Wandering by lone seabreakers,
> And sitting by desolate streams;
> World-losers and world-forsakers,
> On whom the pale moon gleams:
> *Yet we are the movers and shakers*
> *Of the world for ever, it seems . . .*
> We, in the ages lying
> In the buried past of the earth,
> Built Ninevah with our sighing,
> And Babel itself in our mirth;
> And o'erthrew them with prophesying
> To the old of the new world's worth;
> *For each age is a dream that is dying,*
> *Or one that is coming to birth.*
>
> *Arthur O'Shaughnessy*

PART TWO

The New Imperatives

~

A S WE HAVE SEEN IN PART ONE, in the present critical phase of the macroshift new ways of thinking and acting are urgently required. We need new values, more up-to-date beliefs, better insight into current trends and possibilities, and a deeper sense of personal and professional responsibility. As a broader spectrum of the population embraces this new mindset, personal creativity will encourage civic and institutional reform. In a basically democratic world, the way to navigate a macroshift is not by top-down decision making but by bottom-up initiative and grassroots support.

In Part Two we consider the values, beliefs, and ethics that can bring our macroshift to a humane and sustainable conclusion. These "soft" factors in the life of society are the new imperatives of our time—they are even more essential to success than the traditional "hard" factors of economic, political, and business engineering and reengineering.

5

Forget Obsolete Beliefs

PERHAPS THE FIRST OF THE NEW IMPERATIVES of our time is to forget obsolete beliefs. To make room for the new, we must do away with the old. Of course, forgetting is not an easy task; in some ways it is even more difficult than learning. But if what we have in our mind conflicts with what we should get *into* it, selective forgetting becomes necessary. This is the case in regard to a number of present-day values and beliefs.

The Principal Malign Myths

We begin with five "malign myths" that we should promptly forget. Though obsolete and now even dangerous, they still command attention and determine behavior.

THE FIRST MYTH:
"NATURE IS INEXHAUSTIBLE"

The belief that, for all practical intents and purposes, the environment around us is an infinite source of resources and an infinite sink of wastes is a persistent myth. Its origins go back to the archaic empires. It would hardly have occurred to the inhabitants of ancient Babylonia, Sumer, Egypt, India, or China that the environment around them could ever be exhausted of the basic necessities of life—edible plants, domestic animals, clean water, and breathable air—or fouled by dumping wastes and garbage. Nature must have appeared far too vast to be tainted, polluted, or defiled by what humans did in their tiny settlements, and on the lands that surrounded them.

> ⌁ *In a globally extended industrial civilization wielding powerful technologies, the belief in the inexhaustibility of nature is not only patently false but extremely dangerous. . . . If we persist in this belief, we will end up with an impoverished environment incapable of supplying the resources required by our rapidly growing populations.* ⌁

The myth of an inexhaustible environment inspired a millennia-old trend. In many parts of Africa, Asia, and pre-Colombian America human communities had a deep respect for the environment and used only as much as nature could regenerate, but innovation-oriented civilizations tended to overexploit their environment. The Mycenean and Olmec civilizations and those of the Indus Valley are notable examples. In the Fertile Crescent this has had long-lasting consequences. Here, at the cradle of Western civilization, humans were not content with the perennial rhythms and cycles of nature but sought ways to harness nature to serve their own ends. The land, though hot and arid in spots, appeared amenable to exploitation. In some places, such as ancient Sumer, flash floods would wash away irrigation channels and dams, leaving fields arid, but elsewhere, as in the Nile Valley, the environment was relatively benign. Great rivers irrigated the land, brought in silt, and washed away wastes. Not surprisingly, the archaic civilizations were riverine civilizations, built on the shores of the Nile, the Tigris-Euphrates, the Ganges, the Huang-Ho, and the Yellow rivers.

The naive, if at the time comprehensible, belief in the inexhaustibility of nature made much of the Fertile Crescent of biblical times into the Middle East of today—a region with vast areas of arid and infertile land. It did not, however, produce entirely catastrophic consequences. People could move on, colonizing new lands and exploiting fresh resources. Today there is nowhere left to go. In a globally extended industrial civilization wielding powerful technologies, the belief in the inexhaustibility of nature is not only patently false but extremely dangerous. It gives free rein to the overuse and thoughtless impairment of the natural resources of the planet and the unreflective overload of the biosphere's self-regenerative capacities. If we persist in this belief, we will end up with an impoverished environment incapable of supplying the resources required by our rapidly growing populations.

THE SECOND MYTH:
"NATURE IS A GIANT MECHANISM"

The second malign myth dates from the early modern age, a carryover from the Galilean-Newtonian view of the world, where simple causes have direct and simple effects. The idea of nature as a giant mechanism is well adapted to creating and operating medieval technologies such as watermills and windmills, pumps, mechanical clocks, and animal-drawn plows and carriages, but it fails when it comes to jet turbines, nuclear reactors, networked computers, and genetically engineered plants and microbes. Sophisticated technologies do not work like Newtonian machines, and they do not have directly calculable effects.

    ∼ *Twentieth-century industrial civilization persisted in treating both its technologies and its natural environment as a kind of mechanism that can be engineered and reengineered. The result is the rapid and largely unforeseen degradation of water, air, and soil and the progressive impairment of local and continental ecosystems.* ∼

Yet, when all is said and done, the belief that nature can be engineered like a machine persists. The basic notion is that doing one thing can always be relied upon to lead predictably to another thing—as pressing a key on an old-fashioned typewriter causes an arm to lift and print the corresponding letter on a sheet of paper. On the modern computer, however, sophisticated programs interpret the information entered on the keyboard and decide the result. The mechanistic concept works even less well when man-made technologies interface with nature. The way a transplanted gene is expressed in one plant is foreseeable as regards that plant, but it is problematic when it comes to the interaction of that plant with its environment. The same gene that produces the foreseen and desired effect in the transgenic plant can produce unforeseen and undesirable effect in different species. "Horizontal gene-transfer" is always a possibility, and its long-term consequences for the wider ecosystem are unpredictable. These consequences may prove disastrous for the integrity of nature as well as for the yield of agricultural lands.

Nonetheless, twentieth-century industrial civilization held to the rationality of modern-age Logos and persisted in treating both its technologies and its natural environment as a kind of mechanism that can be engineered and reengineered. The result is the rapid and largely unforeseen degradation of water, air, and soil and the progressive impairment of local and continental ecosystems. The myth of nature as a mechanism, though only centuries rather than millennia old, is obsolete and is already clearly counterproductive.

THE THIRD MYTH:
"LIFE IS A STRUGGLE FOR SURVIVAL"

This myth dates from the nineteenth century, a consequence of the popularity of Darwin's theory of natural selection. It claims that in society, as in nature, "the fittest survive." This is taken to mean that if we want to survive we have to be fit for the existential struggle—at least fitter than others around us. In the context of society, life is considered a competition for precious and sometimes scarce resources where fitness is not determined by the genes but is a personal and cultural trait, such as smartness, daring, ambition, and the political and financial means to put them to work.

> ∽ *In our day the consequences of social Darwinism go beyond armed aggression to the more subtle, but in some ways equally merciless, struggle of competitors in the marketplace. . . . States and entire populations are relegated to the role of clients and consumers and, if poor, dismissed as marginal factors in the equations that determine success in the global marketplace.* ∽

Transposing nineteenth-century Darwinism into the sphere of society is dangerous, as the "social Darwinism" embraced by Hitler's Nazi ideology has shown. It justified the conquest of territories in the name of creating more *Lebensraum* (living space) and the subjugation of other peoples in the name of racial fitness and purity. In our day the consequences of social Darwinism go beyond armed aggression to the more subtle, but in some ways equally merciless, struggle of competitors in the marketplace. Carried out mercilessly, it produces widening gaps between rich and poor and concentrates wealth and power in the hands of corporate managers and international financiers. States and entire populations are relegated to the role of clients and consumers and, if poor, dismissed as marginal factors in the equations that determine success in the global marketplace.

The Fourth Myth:
"The Market Distributes Benefits"

The fourth malign myth is directly related to the third—indeed, it serves as its moral justification. Unlike in nature, where the consequence of "fitness" is the spread and dominance of the fit species and the extinction or marginalization of the rest, in society there is said to be a mechanism that distributes the profits instead of having them accrue uniquely to the "fit." This is the market, governed by what Adam Smith called the "invisible hand." It acts equitably: if I do well for myself, I benefit not only myself, my family, and my company but also my community. In the economy as a whole, wealth "trickles down" from the rich to the poor. A rising tide, said John Kennedy, lifts all boats.

> ⁓ *The myth of the market leaves out of account that the market distributes benefits only under conditions of near-perfect competition, where all players start with a more or less equal number of chips. . . . in the real world the playing field is never level and favors the winners at the expense of the losers.* ⁓

The myth of the market is comforting; not surprisingly, it is often cited by the winners. Unfortunately it leaves out of account a provision already noted by the classical economists: that the market distributes benefits only under conditions of near-perfect competition, where all players start with a more or less equal number of chips. Nobody has, or ever had, first-hand experience of the market working equitably for all. Unlike in theory, in the real world the playing field is never level, and favors the winners at the expense of the losers. This is evident in the income distribution of the contemporary world where the poorest 40 percent of the population is left with 3 percent of the global wealth, while the wealth of a few hundred billionaires equals the revenue of half the world's population.

THE FIFTH MYTH:
"THE MORE YOU CONSUME THE BETTER YOU ARE"

This is the myth that there is a strict equivalence between the size of your wallet—as demonstrated by the size of your car and the size of your house, among other things—and your personal worth as the owner of the wallet.

The equivalence of human worth with financial worth has been consciously fueled by business. In former years companies did not hesitate to advertise unlimited consumption as a realistic possibility and conspicuous consumption as the ideal. Victor Lebov, a U.S. retailing analyst writing shortly after World War II, put the consumerist philosophy in terms reminiscent of a myth. "Our enormously productive economy," he said, "demands that we make consumption our way of life, that we convert the buying and use of goods into rituals, that we seek our spiritual satisfaction, our ego satisfaction, in consumption. The economy needs things consumed, burned, worn out, replaced, and discarded at an ever-increasing rate." The consumption myth was, and to some extent still is, extremely powerful. According to some estimates, the modern world has consumed in constant dollars as many goods and services since 1950 as in all previous generations put together.

⌒ The consequences and side effects of consumerism were not known in the 1950s but they are widely known today. . . . Yet the myth that one is a better, indeed a more superior person when one owns more and uses more is persistent. ⌒

Not only are there more people who consume in the world, on average they also consume far more. This trend cannot be sustained. The consequences and side effects of consumerism were not known in the 1950s, but they are widely known today. Overconsumption affects physical health and mental equilibrium alike. Yet the myth that one is a better, indeed a more superior person when one owns more and uses more is persistent. This is not as frankly admitted today as it was in the past, but in many ways the marketing of houses, cars, and consumer goods is still counting on it—and with good reason.

Lesser Beliefs Best Forgotten

In addition to the five malign myths, a number of less entrenched and dangerous beliefs are equally ripe for the dust heap. Here are a few of them:

Order through hierarchy: Order in society can only be achieved by rules and laws and their proper enforcement, and this requires a chain of command that is recognized and obeyed by all. A few people on top (mostly males) make up the rules, legislate the laws, give the orders, and ensure compliance with them. Everyone else is to obey the rules and take his and her place within the social and political order.

The ideology of Westfalia: The formally constituted nation-state is the sole political reality. It is the only entity that has true sovereignty, as the legal conventions coming into force at the Peace of Westfalia specified. These conventions confer on nation-states the "inalienable right" to have an independent government, internationally recognized boundaries, a national currency and a national army, diplomatic relations with other states, and action free from fetters within their own borders.

Everyone is unique and separate: We are all unique and separate individuals enclosed by our skin and pursuing our own interests. The same as our country, we have only ourselves to rely on; everyone else is either friend or foe, at best linked to us by ties of mutual (but alas mostly short-term) interest.

Everything is reversible: The problems we experience are temporary interludes of perturbation after which everything goes back to normal. All we need to do is manage the difficulties that crop up using tried and tested methods of problem solving and, if necessary, crisis management. Business as unusual has evolved out of business as usual, and sooner or later will reverse back into it.

These beliefs are obsolete and they, too, can turn dangerous. The reasons are not difficult to perceive. Male-dominated hierarchies do not work well even in the Army and the Church, much less in business and society. Leading managers have already learned the advantages of lean structures and teamwork, but for the most part social and political institutions still operate in the traditional hierarchical mode. As a result, governments tend to be heavy handed, and their workings are cumbersome and inefficient.

Admitting nothing but our own nation-state as the focus of allegiance is a mistaken form of patriotism. It can lead to chauvinism and intolerance and to periodic excesses by dictatorial regimes characterized by armed aggression and ethnic cleansing.

Seeing ourselves as separate from the social and the natural world in which we live could convert natural impulses to seek our own advantage into a short-sighted struggle among ever more desperate and unequal competitors. This is a dangerous path to follow, both for individuals and for the country in which they live.

No experience of shocks and crises can change our perceptions if we remain convinced that the problems we encounter are but temporary disturbances in an unchanging and perhaps unchangeable status quo. This obsolete belief can constrain innovative change that would have broad benefits throughout the world.

Underlying these persistent beliefs are a number of flawed conceptions. Let's examine six of these widespread assumptions.

My country, right or wrong. Come what may, we owe allegiance only to one flag and one government.

The cult of efficiency. We must get the maximum out of every person, every machine, and every organization regardless of what is produced and whether or not it serves a useful purpose.

The technological imperative. Anything that can be done ought to be done. If it can be made or performed, it can be sold, and if it is sold, it is good for us and the economy.

Newer is better. Anything that is new is better than (almost) anything that is last year's.

Economic rationality. The value of everything, including human
beings, can be calculated in money. What everybody wants is to
get rich. The rest is idle conversation or simple pretense.

The future is none of our business. Why should we worry about the
good of the next generation? Every generation has to look after
itself.

Why these conceptions are misleading can also be spelled out.
The chauvinistic assertion "my country, right or wrong" plays
untold havoc both domestically and internationally, calling for people to fight for causes a new government later repudiates, to espouse
the values and worldviews of a small group of political leaders, and
to ignore the growing cultural, social, and economic ties that evolve
among people in different parts of the globe.

Efficiency without regard to what is produced and whom it will
benefit leads to mounting unemployment, catering to the demands
of the rich without regard to the needs of the poor, and polarization
of society into "monetized" and "traditional" sectors.

The technological imperative results in a plethora of goods that
people only think they need; some of them they use actually at their
peril.

That newer would always be better is simply not true. Often, the
newer is worse—more expensive, more wasteful, more damaging to
health, and more polluting, alienating, or stressful.

The naive reduction of everything and everybody to economic
value may have seemed rational during epochs in which a great economic upswing turned all heads and pushed everything else into
the background, but it is foolhardy at a time when people are beginning to rediscover deep-rooted social and spiritual values and to
cultivate lifestyles of voluntary simplicity.

Finally, living without conscious forward planning—though it
may have been fine in days of rapid growth when each new gener-

ation could ensure a good life for itself—is not a responsible option at a time when the decisions we make today will have a profound impact on the well-being of those who come after us.

Forgetting these and related beliefs does not mean giving up all myths and beliefs. Myths themselves are cultural beliefs, and they can orient human aspiration. As anthropologist Joseph Campbell pointed out, myths can explain the world, guide individual development, and provide shared direction. But myths can also turn sour, outliving their usefulness. When that happens, it is in society's interest to forget them. Countless myths have become obsolete. In Central America dozens of Mayan temples lie abandoned; in Peru countless Incan monuments are scattered in ruins. Celtic cairns in Wales, Khmer statues in Kampuchea, Sumerian ziggurats in Iraq, and giant stone heads on Easter Island are all mute witnesses of once flowering systems of belief that have disappeared either because they misguided their people or because more viable systems appeared in their midst.

*   *   *   *   *   *   *   *

The first of the new imperatives of our time should now be evident: Forget the beliefs that are not "in sync" with your world—beliefs that no longer serve your life, and the life of others around you.

6

Learn to Live with Diversity

FORGETTING THE MYTHS that no longer serve us is essential, but in itself it is not enough. We must also adopt values and beliefs that are better in tune with our world. It is to these that we now turn.

> ⌁ *People in the United States and Europe tend to think that everybody wants to live and be like them, . . . but a great deal of diversity remains in people's views of themselves, of society, of nature, and of freedom and justice. . . . Notwithstanding the spread of MacDonaldism, worldwide Coca-Colonization, the Internet, and the emergence of global markets, the contemporary world is becoming more rather than less diverse.* ⌁

The cultural diversity of the contemporary world is frequently underestimated. People in the United States and Europe tend to think that everybody wants to live and be like them—the rest is but sophistry and pretense. It is true that the level of consumption, material aspirations and technology, and the values of the industrialized world are dominant, but a great deal of diversity remains in people's views of themselves, of society, of nature, and of freedom and justice. Disregarding, or just underestimating, the world's cultural diversity produced blood-baths in Ireland, the Middle East, the Arab world, sub-Saharan Africa, Latin America, the Indian subcontinent, and Southeast Asia.

The disregard of entrenched cultural differences also led to the Yugoslav cataclysm that erupted in 1999. In the Balkans two different cultures have coexisted since Constantine divided the Roman Empire: the Roman Catholic and the Greek Orthodox. When the Ottomans entered Bosnia in the fifteenth century, these two cultures were joined by a third: Islam. They clashed time and time again. Tito's fight, first against the Nazi invaders and then against the imperialistic Soviet superpower, unified the clashing factions, but when Tito died and the external enemy vanished, ethnic animosities erupted again. A recognition of these cultural factors could have led to a better policy in regard to the Serb leadership than armed intervention by foreign powers.

Whether in the Balkans, in the Middle East, or elsewhere in the Southern Hemisphere, there is a need for a better understanding of the differences that mark today's cultures and ethnic groups. Notwithstanding the spread of MacDonaldisms, worldwide Coca-Colonization, the Internet, and the emergence of global markets, the contemporary world is becoming more rather than less diverse. In the southern half of the Americas, for example, a new brand of cultural nationalism is emerging. Latin Americans resent their dependence on North America and also resent being receivers rather than producers of the cultural currents that shape the contemporary world. Foreign cultural domination is an agonizing issue for Arabs as well, who perceive it as an element of Western hegemony vis-à-vis their countries. They find themselves at the passive end of an intercultural dialogue that links them almost exclusively with Western Europe and North America. Militant fundamentalism is an extreme expression of the resentment generated by these conditions.

India and the countries of South Asia have had prolonged contact with British culture, but despite their admiration and assimilation of many of its traits, these cultures are intent on protecting their own heritage. In Russia, in turn, historical experience has made for a profound ambivalence regarding Western culture, an attitude that persists to this day. Its main elements are admiration for the achievements of the West in technology as well as in high culture and fear that these achievements will overwhelm the Russian cultural heritage and the identity it bestows on people.

Admiration mixed with fear is also a hallmark of the cultures of the young nations of sub-Saharan Africa. Though avid consumers of industrial culture, some Africans are increasingly intent on fortifying their own cultural heritage. While the poor segment of the population remains steeped in traditional beliefs and ways of life, a small élite of intellectuals searches for the roots of African racial identity and a still smaller élite of political leaders is concerned above all with its people's national identity.

Contrasts with the Western way of seeing oneself and the world, though not always recognized, surface on every continent. Latin Americans have a more highly developed sense of spirituality than the people of North America. This has historical roots, with transcendentalist elements of Latin culture dating back to the fifteenth century. Throughout the South American continent the Catholic scholasticism of the European Middle Ages was more than a monastic philosophy: it was a cognitive system intrinsic to state and society that governed every aspect of life. Subservience to ecclesiastical authority, like subservience to God and King, became axiomatic in the morality of everyday life. Even when the colonial epoch drew to a close, no accommodation took place between the scholastic legacy and modern scientific thought. Anglo-Saxon pragmatism, rooted in the application of the concepts and methods of the natural sciences to the material spheres of life, has never taken hold in the Latin parts of the hemisphere.

Though in a different form, transcendentalism is also a feature of the Hindu and Buddhist cultures of the Indian subcontinent. It focuses people's attention on spiritual matters and functions as a counterweight to the rising materialism and consumerism of the "modernized" sector. In the Muslim culture, transcendentalism combines with monotheism, and in Sufism it acquires a mystical streak. Mysticism is prevalent also in the indigenous cultures of black Africa. These cultures have always been spiritualistic and animistic, and these features have not been eliminated in the traditional sectors of the population by the zeal of Christian missionaries, nor have they been overcome by the marketing propaganda of transnational corporations.

The Oriental mind conserves many aspects of its traditional beliefs. The great cultural circle that radiated from China during the last millennium was shaped by the naturalism of Lao Tse, the social discipline of Confucius, and the Buddha's quest for personal enlightenment. In the twentieth century these cultural origins branched in different directions, giving rise to the orthodox culture of Mao's Yanan, the pragmatic culture of Hong Kong's Kong-Tai, and the mix of naturalism, Confucianism, and Buddhism that characterizes the culture of contemporary Japan. The Kong-Tai and Japanese branches of the Chinese cultural tradition maintain a penchant for all things concrete and practical, so it is not surprising that societies where these strong traditions have held sway had no difficulty in adopting, or even improving upon, Western technology—even if (as we have seen in chapter 3) they could not avoid the negative consequences of a technology-based market economy. These cultures became "modernized" but not westernized. Oriental work habits, group loyalties, and lifestyles remain culture-specific to this day, and they differ from those current in Europe and North America.

The materialistic individualism and pragmatism of Western culture is not monolithic even in Europe and the United States. It is tempered with religious beliefs centered on the existence of God and a pantheon of saints or prophets. It exhibits a penchant for embracing the five "malignant myths" discussed earlier, together with many of the other beliefs best forgotten. None of these mesh with the reality of the contemporary world; they are articles of faith. Nonetheless, they continue to influence Western people's values and behavior.

Finding unity within the diversity of the contemporary world is essential for assuring the chances of life, or just of survival, for all the people of the human family. One such potential for unity is the need for cooperation among the world's diverse peoples and cultures. The basic resources of the planet—air, water, soil, mineral resources, and energy—must be shared by all people, regardless of their level of industrialization and economic development. But if all people are to have access to these resources, economies, enterprises, and states must not engage in the obsolete strategy of outcompeting each other for access to them. Instead, they must cooperate with each other to ensure that everybody has enough access to live and develop.

Governments and managers need to change their focus from "win-lose" games to "win-win" games where everybody benefits. Many such games can be played. For example, the exploitation, use, and discard of material resources can be structured so that the benefit of one also spells benefit for others. The same goes for the use of the planet's atmosphere, soils, and energy sources. Family planning and the environment are certainly areas where both sides can win: an environment with modest population growth offers better access to resources for everyone.

~ A peaceful and sustainable world is not built by eliminating cultural differences but by cooperation that makes productive use of them. ~

National and international security have often been considered a playing field for win-lose games. If I win by conquering you, your territory, your people, and your resources, you lose in all these respects. Yet in the contemporary world of interdependence, peace and security are a requirement for all people, and assuring them is of benefit to everyone. As we shall see in chapter 8, cooperation in the area of collective peacekeeping can create a more solid foundation for peace and security than mutual distrust balanced by armed forces.

The way to play win-win games is to:

- share useful skills, technologies, and capital with poorer or less developed partners;

- channel investment into education, communication, human resource development and economic and social infrastructure;

- create a joint peacekeeping system instead of investing in nuclear, biological, chemical, and conventional weapons;

- have fewer children in rapidly growing high-fertility populations; and

- respect the balances and thresholds that are vital to the integrity of nature.

A peaceful and sustainable world is not built by eliminating cultural differences but by cooperation that makes productive use of them.

* * * * * * * *

The second of the new imperatives of our time is to recognize, respect, and through win-win strategies make proper use of the diversity of the cultures, nations, and peoples of today's world.

7

Embrace a Planetary Ethic

VALUES AND BELIEFS determine the way we perceive the world
and suggest the ways we prioritize the responses to our perceptions. They affect almost all areas of our judgment and behavior.
However, in the wider context of society individual values and beliefs
are unlikely to conform to a common standard. If mutually consistent values and beliefs are not to be imposed "from above," a further
factor needs to be present. This is a shared ethic: the acceptance of
a common morality. In an interdependent world, this ethic must be
shared by the entire human family; it must be a *planetary* ethic.

> *A planetary ethic respects the conditions under which all peo-
> ple in the world community can live in dignity and freedom, with-
> out destroying each other's chances of livelihood, culture, society, and
> environment.*

A planetary ethic is a major imperative of our time. We all have
our private morality: our personal ethic. This varies with the personality, the ambitions, and the circumstances of each of us. It
reflects our unique background, heritage, and family and community situation. We also have a public morality, the ethic shared in
our community, ethnic group, state or nation. This is the ethic the
group in which we live requires of us in order for it to function. It

reflects its culture, social structure, economic development, and environmental conditions. But there is also a universal morality—a planetary ethic. This is the ethic the human family as a whole requires so that all its members can live and develop.

Universal morality is an essential part of private and public morality. It respects the conditions under which all people in the world community can live in dignity and freedom, without destroying each other's chances of livelihood, culture, society, and environment. It does not prescribe the nature of our private and public morality—it only ensures that they do not give rise to behaviors that are damaging to the planetary community that is the vital context of our lives.

How could a morality shared the world over arise and spread in society? Traditionally, setting the norms of morality was the task of the religions. The Ten Commandments of Jews and Christians, the provisions for the faithful in Islam, and the Rules of Right Livelihood of the Buddhists are examples. Today the dominance of science has reduced the power of religious doctrines to regulate human behavior, and many people look to science for practical guidance. Yet scientists, with some notable exceptions, discover few principles that would provide a basis for universal morality. Saint-Simon in the late 1700s, Auguste Comte in the early 1800s, and Émile Durkheim in the late 1800s and early 1900s all tried to develop "positive" scientific observation- and experiment-based principles for a meaningful and publicly acceptable ethic. This endeavor, as a whole, however, was so foreign to science's commitment to value neutrality and objectivity that it was not taken up by mainstream twentieth-century scientists.

Today scientists as well as political leaders are recognizing the need for principles that would suggest universal norms of behavior. In April 1990 in the "Universal Declaration of Human Responsibilities," the InterAction Council, a group of twenty-four former heads of state or government, expressed this conviction: "Because global interdependence demands that we must live with each other in harmony, human beings need rules and constraints. Ethics are the minimum standards that make a collective life possible. Without ethics and self-restraint that are their result, humankind would revert to the survival of the fittest. The world is in need of an ethical base on which to stand."

The Union of Concerned Scientists, an organization of leading scientists, concurred. "A new ethic is required," claimed a statement signed in 1993 by 1670 scientists from seventy countries including 102 Nobel laureates. "This ethic must motivate a great movement, convincing reluctant leaders and reluctant governments and reluctant peoples themselves to effect the needed changes." The scientists noted our new responsibility for caring for the Earth and warned that "a great change in our stewardship of the Earth and the life on it is required if vast human misery is to be avoided and our global home on this planet is not to be irretrievably mutilated." Human beings and the natural world, they said, are on a collision course. This may so alter the living world that it will be unable to sustain life as we know it.

Undoubtedly the time has come to give serious attention to a morality that can be embraced by all people regardless of their creed, religion, race, sex, or secular belief. It must have intuitive appeal, addressing the basic moral instinct present in all healthy individuals. This merits serious thought. Because the egalitarian ideals of Marx, Lenin, and Mao failed in practice in communist countries, the highest expression of everyday ethics for the great bulk of humanity has been liberalism, the conceptual heritage of Bentham, Locke, and Hume, the classical school of British philosophers. Here ethics and morality have no objective basis: human actions are based on self-interest, moderated at best by an element of altruistic sympathy. People are not to be prevented from pursuing their self-interest as long as they observe the rules that permit life in civilized society. "Live and let live" is the liberal principle. You can live in any way you please, as long as you do not break any laws.

In practice the liberal morality is less liberal than this. It allows people to live as they please not only as long as they do not break any laws but as long as they do not interfere with my living as I please. Live as you please—but preferably not in my backyard.

⁓ Letting everyone live as they please as long as they keep both within the law and out of my backyard entails a serious risk. We can no longer keep others out of our backyard—we live in a crowded and interdependent world. And it is becoming dangerous to let everybody live in any way they want. ⁓

In today's world classical liberalism makes for a misplaced form of tolerance. Letting everyone live as they please as long as they keep both within the law and out of my backyard entails a serious risk. We can no longer keep others out of our backyard—we live in a crowded and interdependent world. And it is becoming dangerous to let everybody live in any way they want. The rich and the powerful could consume a disproportionate share of the resources to which we, too, have a legitimate claim, and both rich and poor could inflict irreversible damage on the environment that we have to share with them.

Rather than "live and let live," we need a planetary ethic that is just as intuitively meaningful and instinctively appealing as the ethic of liberalism but better adapted to current conditions on this planet. Such an ethic would substitute for liberalism's "Live and let live" Gandhi's "Live more simply, so others can simply live." This idea needs further refinement, however, because we are not concerned with the intrinsic simplicity of lifestyles but with their impact on society and nature. This must not exceed the capacity of the planet to provide for the needs of all its inhabitants. In consequence we can encapsulate the planetary ethic in the following principle: "Live in a way that allows others to live as well."

The Planetary Enlargement of Traditional Ethics

In the principle "live in a way that allows others to live as well" the concept of "others" refers not only to humans but to all the plants and animals and all the living beings that make up the planet's web of life.

This is comparatively new in the history of Western moral philosophy. For virtually the entire duration of the intellectual history of this hemisphere, ethical discussion failed to show a direct concern with obligations toward nature. Plants and animals were assigned indirect, instrumental value, according to whether they contributed to, or detracted from, the realization of the values of human life and well-being. Intrinsic values—values that pertain to things in virtue of their own being and characteristics—have been assigned only to humans. Human life, as Immanuel Kant made clear, is always an end in itself and never a means to some other end. Consequently moral obligations were limited to family, friends, and fellow citizens—to the moral community of humans.

Subsequently moral commitments have been extended to all the communities of humans and, with recent debates regarding our responsibility for the future, to future generations as well. But until very recently, nonhuman nature was excluded from the sphere of beings toward which we have moral commitments. Animals were generally perceived as significantly different from, and inferior to, human beings. They were seen to lack some essential quality: reason or moral agency, language or self-awareness, even consciousness. For this reason they were excluded from the moral community that defines the range of moral obligations.

By the mid-1970s this concept had been contested. Australian moral philosopher Peter Singer drew an explicit parallel between women's liberation and the movement to "liberate" animals. Animal liberation, he said, is the next step in the evolution of people's moral sensibility. Whether they are human or nonhuman, all animals are equal.

In the opinion of an increasing number of contemporary thinkers—led by the school of "deep ecology" founded by Norwegian philosopher Arne Naess—the moral community must also include nonhuman forms of life. This community is defined not as the community of beings who have a moral consciousness (for that would limit it to humans) but as the community of beings toward whom moral humans have duties.

Scores of books and articles have been written acknowledging the moral status and intrinsic value of animals and defining our duties toward them. The idea of an ethic that recognizes human duties and obligations toward all forms of life is becoming accepted as a basic tenet of contemporary morality.

Living in ways that enable others to live as well is the planetary ethic of our time—but is it practicable? Will it be accepted and embraced by a significant segment of society? This question will not be decided by moral philosophers but by processes within democratic societies. The times when kings, popes, and princes could decide what is moral and what is not are over. In today's world, principles regulating people's behavior come from the people themselves.

Thomas Jefferson said, if you believe that the people are not sufficiently informed to exercise the power of *demos* in society, the democratic solution is not to take power from their hands but to inform them. Informing others of the requirement for an ethic adapted to our time is not a quixotic endeavor. If people realize that there is a real need for a planetary ethic, and that abiding by it does not dictate the nature of our private and public morality, or entail undue sacrifice, they will respond with interest and alacrity.

The need for a planetary ethic is real, and it can be made evident. Human life is intimately tied to the lives of other species, in fact, to the entire biosphere. If we continue to interfere with the ecological balance established among the diverse species, conditions in the biosphere will evolve along pathways distinctly inhospitable to humankind's well-being and threatening for its survival. Agricultural lands will erode, weather patterns will turn hostile, water tables will fall and ocean levels rise, lethal radiation will penetrate the atmosphere, and micro-organisms fundamentally incompatible with our organism will proliferate. A wide variety of ecocatastrophes will come about.

We can also make clear that abiding by a planetary ethic does not entail particular sacrifices. Living in a way that enables others in the biosphere to live as well does not mean being self-denying: we can continue to strive for excellence and beauty, personal growth and enjoyment, even for comfort and luxury. But in the context of a planetary ethic the pleasures and achievements of life are defined in relation to the quality of enjoyment and level of satisfaction they provide rather than in terms of the amount of money they cost and the quantity of materials and energy they require. This ethic requires that we take into account the basic question, "Is how I live and what I do compatible with the right to life of others?" Does it allow access to the basic resources of life for six or more billion humans and for the plants and animals that populate our life-supporting environment?

These questions must be answered by each of us in regard to everything we do. They can be answered using a basic rule of thumb: *envisage the consequences of your action on the life and activity of others*. Does it, or does it not, rob basic resources from them? Does it, or does it not, despoil their environment? These questions are not impossible to answer. By way of example, let's look at three of the most widespread practices in the contemporary world: eating meat, smoking, and the use of the private automobile.

THE MORALITY OF EATING MEAT, SMOKING, AND DRIVING

EATING MEAT

Cutting back on our consumption of meat is both a sustainability and a health imperative. World meat consumption has risen from 44 million tons in 1950 to 217 million tons by 1999, nearly a fivefold increase—an untenable trend. In addition, the meat we buy today is not the safe meat grandmother bought in 1950. Quite aside from the danger of it being infected by mad-cow disease, it is likely to contain progesterone, testosterone, avoparcin, and clenbuterol—chemicals farmers pump into cattle to fatten them up and keep them healthy. Anabolic steroids, growth hormones, and beta-agonists turn fat into muscle; antibiotics stimulate growth and protect sedentary animals against diseases they would not get if they were kept in more natural conditions.

A diet based on heavy meat eating is not only unhealthy, it is immoral: it indulges a personal fancy at the expense of depleting resources essential to feed the entire human population. Red meat comes from cattle, and cattle must be fed. The grain fed to cattle is removed from human consumption. If cows returned equivalent nutrition in the form of meat, their feed would not be wasted. But the calorific energy provided by beef is only one-seventh of the energy of the feed.

This means that in the process of converting grain into beef, cows "waste" six-sevenths of the nutritional value of the planet's primary produce. The proportion is more favorable in poultry: an average chicken uses only two-thirds of the calorific value of the feed it consumes.

There is simply not enough grain to feed all the animals that would be needed to supply meat for the tables of the world's entire population. These giant herds of cattle and endless farms of poultry would require more grain than the total output of the agricultural lands—according to some calculations, about twice as much. Given the amount of land available for farming and the known and presently used agricultural methods, doubling today's grain production would call for economically prohibitive investments. The rational and moral solution is to phase out the mass-production of cattle and poultry—not by massive slaughter but by breeding fewer animals and breeding them healthier.

The nutritive needs of the world's population can be satisfied by eating more vegetables and grain and less meat, using first and foremost the produce of one's own country, region, and environment. Grain- and plant-based food self-reliance provides a healthier diet, and it allows the world's economically exploitable agricultural lands to be worked to satisfy the needs of the whole of the human family.

SMOKING

What goes for meat eating also goes for smoking. The fact that smoking is dangerous to health can be read on every packet of cigarettes, but it is not generally known that growing tobacco for export robs millions of poor people of fertile land on which they could grow cereals and vegetables. As long as there is a market for tobacco exports, agribusinesses and profit-hungry farmers will plant tobacco instead of wheat, corn, or soy. The market for tobacco exports will remain as long as large numbers of people continue to smoke. Tobacco, together with other cash crops such as coffee and tea, commands a considerable portion of the world's fertile lands, yet no such produce is a true necessity.

Reducing the demand for red meat, coffee and tea, and tobacco would mean a healthier life for the rich and a chance for adequate nourishment for the poor. A better pattern of land use would permit feeding six, eight, or even ten billion people without conquering new land and engaging in risky experiments with genetically manipulated crop varieties. With today's consumption patterns, on the other hand, the world's agricultural lands can barely feed the human population. It takes only 1 acre of productive land to provide the average Indian's agriculture-related needs, but satisfying the needs of a typical American takes fully 12 acres. Making 12 acres of productive land available for all six billion people alive today would require two more planets the size of Earth.

DRIVING

According to a World Bank estimate, by the year 2010 the population of motor vehicles will swell to one billion. Unless there is a rapid shift to new fuel tech-nologies—which is possible, but difficult to achieve worldwide—doubling the cur-rent motor vehicle energy requirements would double the level of smog precursors and greenhouse gases. Cars and trucks would choke the streets of third world cities and the transportation arteries of developing regions. This level of motor vehicle use is not a necessity in either the industrialized or the devel-oping world. For goods transport, rails and rivers could be more effectively used, and for city dwellers, public transportation could be pressed into wide-scale service, reducing the number of private vehicles. In most cases this would reduce the material standard of living but not the quality of life.

Being moral in our day means thinking twice before taking one's car to town when public transport is available. It means taking pride in clean and well-kept subways, trams, and buses, and traveling sociably in the company of others rather than in the air-conditioned and telephone and hi-fi equipped isolation of a private automobile. If one is physically fit, short trips by bicycle make for a hap-pier choice still: besides saving fuel, reducing traffic congestion, and cutting down on pollution, one benefits from an extra dose of fresh air and exercise.

We know that the urban sprawl created by the widespread use of private auto-mobiles is undesirable, that traffic jams are frustrating and counter-productive, and that the gasoline-powered internal combustion engine uses up finite resources and contributes to air pollution and global warming. Today there are perfectly good alternatives to the classic automobile: cars running on natural gas, fuel cells, compressed air, or liquid hydrogen, to mention but a few. Yet people continue to demand and use gasoline-powered cars. As long as the demand keeps up, industries will not introduce the alternative fuels and cities and states will not procure cleaner and more efficient public transportation.

The switch from the liberal morality of classical industrial society to a more global and responsible ethic is slow in coming; the outdated precept "live and let live (though not, of course, in my backyard)" persists. For the most part, affluent people still live in a way that reduces the chances for the poor to achieve an acceptable quality of life. If all people used and overused private cars, smoked, ate a heavy meat diet, and used the myriad appliances that go with the affluent lifestyle, many of the essential resources of the planet would be rapidly exhausted and its self-generative powers would be drastically reduced.

Clearly, the poor people of the world must also adopt a planetary ethic. If they persist in pursuing the values and lifestyles of the affluent, little will be gained. It is not enough for well-to-do Americans, Europeans, and Japanese to reduce harmful industrial, residential, and transportation emissions and cut down on gross energy consumption. If the Chinese, the Indian, and other poor country populations continue to burn coal for electricity and wood for cooking, implement classical Industrial Age economic policies, and acquire Western living, driving, and consumer habits, nothing will be gained. Only if a critical mass of people of the contemporary world adopt a planetary ethic do we have a realistic chance of creating a world where the right to life and well-being is assured for all and the human impact on the environment does not exceed the self-regenerative capacities of the biosphere.

* * * * * * * *

The third element of the new imperative is now before us: Embrace a planetary ethic—live in a way that enables all others to live as well.

8

Meet Your Responsibilities

OBSERVING THE PRINCIPLE "live in a way that enables all others to live as well" means respecting the intrinsic right to life and well-being of all the people and all the things that inhabit the planet. But rights without responsibilities are empty claims. Rights are meaningful only when people meet the responsibilities entailed by those rights.

There are specific responsibilities attached to human rights in all spheres of life and action: the personal sphere, the business sphere, and the civic or political sphere. Observing them constitutes the last, but by no means the least, of the new imperatives of our time.

Personal Responsibilities

The responsibilities that face us in the personal sphere of our life are no longer our private business. They are crucial for the outcome of today's macroshift, and hence they are everybody's business.

Our common future will depend in large measure on the lifestyle and consumption choices we make today. Fortunately, these choices are not difficult to make; a simple rule of thumb applies again. It is a refinement of the much-cited adage, "think globally, act locally." Global thinking remains a key element, but the nature of the local action needs to be specified. What one individual does influences others and can spread to the far corners of the world. Therefore, it is not just action, but *moral* action that is required.

Hardly anything we do in this world is purely local, and as ecologist Garret Hardin said, we can never do "just one thing." Therefore, the criterion of responsibility for our actions must be *Think globally, act morally.*

We have already discussed what moral action means. Now let's consider the concept of global thinking. Global thinking is not utopian, and it is not reserved for an elite few. It is not thinking in general categories, or in millions and billions, whether of humans, hectares, or barrels of oil. It is thinking in terms of processes rather than structures, in terms of dynamic wholes rather than static parts. Its benefit is not to obtain a catalog of ready-made blueprints for making proper choices in any and all circumstances; rather, it is to acquire the perspective by which we can make wise choices of our own.

Thinking in new and in better adapted ways is a uniquely human capability. In the higher animals basic survival-related behavior remains guided by instinct, and instinct changes slowly through the processes of genetic mutation and natural selection. The dominance of experience over instinct is what distinguishes the rapid cultural evolution of humans from the slower genetic evolution of animals. We can learn from experience, and our conscious assessment of experience can steer our behavior, transcending our inherited instincts. When we learn from the experience of the critical phase of today's macroshift, we begin to think globally.

Metaphorically, global thinking means seeing the forest and not just the trees. There are cases, however, in which the metaphor also holds literally. One such case is when a person who does not think globally sees only trees—those of the Brazilian rainforest, for example. He sees the rainforest and sees that Brazil's government is in need of foreign exchange. He also sees bulldozer operators and ranchers in need of work, transporters in need of cargo, hamburger franchises in need of meat, and consumers wanting hamburgers. A globally thinking person sees the whole picture. He sees that the disappearance of trees in the rainforest triggers the loss of topsoil, which leads to changing weather patterns, which in turn lead to advancing deserts and loss of oxygen. He realizes that this creates a vicious cycle that can destroy the rainforests, impoverishing the soils exposed by cutting down the trees, reducing the flow of lumber and beef from the region, making the industries depending on them noncompetitive, and undercutting consumer demand for the corresponding products.

Global thinking informs the choices we make in the private as well as the professional spheres of our lives. When we choose consumer products for our personal use, do we choose fancy items that use a great deal of energy or simple functional devices that do the job with a minimum of waste and fuss? When we choose our work or profession, do we strive to amass the most money in the shortest time or choose to engage in an activity that is meaningful in itself and beneficial to others? Global thinking also enters into the choice of the style we select for our home: do we want a style designed for ostentation or one that inspires coziness and sociability? How we clothe ourselves and our family is likewise informed by considerations of responsibility: do we dress to be conspicuous and to feed our ego, or for genuine self-expression and to preserve family and community values and our cultural heritage?

A CHECKLIST OF PERSONAL MORAL ACTION

◆ Seek simple natural foods, materials, and lifestyles, rejoicing in nature and rejecting uncleanliness, waste, and pollution.

◆ Avoid ostentation in personal appearance, at home and in the workplace, express instead genuine human and cultural values.

◆ Derive satisfaction from making choices that enhance the chances of life and well-being of other people, whether they live in your immediate environment or in distant places.

◆ Be careful not to consume in ways that would prevent the options of others to satisfy the basic needs of life and well-being—not just out of a cool calculation of resource availability and ecological carrying capacity but because of a sense of solidarity with your community, nation and culture, and with the global community of all peoples, nations, and cultures.

Acting in a globally conscious moral way is not difficult, and it does not entail undue sacrifices. When we think globally and act morally, our lives become richer and healthier, and we become better friends and neighbors, less prone to frustration and feelings of guilt. And we have the assurance of thinking and acting as we should, as best we can. More than that no one can ask of us—not, at least, in the personal sphere of our lives.

Business Responsibilities

Thinking globally and acting morally are not the only responsibilities that fall to us. These personal responsibilites are joined by responsibilities in our social and professional spheres. We need to be responsible as managers and collaborators in a business enterprise and as citizens of a country and as members of the global community as well.

Our responsibilities in the business sphere are of particular importance. Business enterprises wield unprecedented power and influence. The top five hundred industrial corporations in the world employ only 0.05 percent of the world's population but control 70 percent of world trade, 80 percent of direct foreign investment, and 25 percent of world economic output. The total sales of the largest twenty corporations exceed the gross domestic product of eighty of the poorest developing countries. The 1998 sales of General Motors, for example, exceeded the gross domestic product of Denmark, Hong Kong, and Poland, as well as of Norway; the sales of Ford and Mitsui exceeded the GDP of South Africa.

The behavior of business enterprises is an important factor influencing the outcome of today's macroshift. This behavior is dictated mainly, but not solely, by economic logic. The culture of enterprise defines the mindset of the leading managers and their staff, and it changes with changes in the business environment. Sometimes ahead of its time, and at other times lagging behind, the culture of enterprise is vital both for the enterprise and for the social and ecological environment in which the enterprise operates. The traditional culture is changing: it had profit and growth on behalf of the shareholders as its centerpiece. The premise was that the business of business is business. Well-made products and services sell themselves—and, if not, marketing is there to create demand for them.

> ～ *In the culture of leading corporations short-term profit seeking has come to be mitigated by concerns with enduring profitability, and unqualified growth seeking has been replaced with a search for a sustainable share in a variety of markets.* ～

This culture is no longer shared by enlightened managers; additional considerations have emerged. Leading managers place increasing emphasis on the philosophy, identity, and role of their enterprise, and the role and ethic of its leadership. In the culture of leading corporations short-term profit seeking has come to be mitigated by concerns with enduring profitability, and unqualified growth seeking has been replaced with a search for a sustainable share in a variety of markets. Notwithstanding the skepticism of some analysts and investors regarding visionary strategies and values-based organizations, and a hard core of resistance to abandoning the "shareholder value is all there is" philosophy, a shift is under way in the culture of leading enterprises from exclusive concern with customers and shareholders to concern with value and with stakeholders. "Every organization needs values," said Jack Welch, chairman of General Electric, "but a lean organization needs them even more." And Ikea chairman Ander Dahlvig noted, "Globalization means stakeholders and responsibilities everywhere."

Concern with value and responsibility for stakeholders cannot be answered by cosmetic solutions. Clients and customers are getting smarter. They are better informed about product quality, price, availability, and service, and more selective about the companies they do business with. Surveys in Europe show that less than 10 percent of the public believes claims of environmental and social responsibility by companies unless they are backed by tangible evidence. Other surveys in the United States indicate that more than 40 percent of consumers say that, when price and quality are comparable, their choice is influenced by the issues they believe are genuinely important to the companies. Market analyses in both Europe and Japan show that high standards and a commitment to social and environmental issues are key factors of competition in an environment where market success means providing higher perceived value at lower price.

There is concrete evidence backing up the research results: more and more investment is flowing into companies that are socially responsible, and with good reason. Socially responsible companies have been doing well and are doing better and better. According to the nonprofit Social Investment Forum, 88 percent of the selective socially conscious investment funds with $100 million or more in assets earned top marks for performance from Morningstar and Lipper Analytical Services through the end of 2000—up from 69 percent at the end of 1999. This kind of performance does not escape the attention of professional fund managers. By the end of 1999 some $2.16 trillion was invested in the United States in socially responsible companies, about 13 percent of the $16.3 trillion under professional management.

No longer an idealistic "soft" factor, social responsibility has become a "hard" dimension of enterprise culture. Some global companies have understood this. Unilever, one of the world's leading users of fish, has hired scientists and developed sophisticated systems to ensure that its fish come from sustainably managed fishing sources; Ikea, a major consumer of wood for furniture, uses the satellite-based information program developed by the World Resources Institute to avoid purchasing wood from endangered areas. Such strategies pay off in share valuation, client and consumer satisfaction, and a healthier and better educated public with higher purchasing power. This is not new. Research by James

Collins and Jerry Porras on the habits of visionary companies has
shown that a common feature of the most successful companies in
the United States for the past one hundred years has been a culture
that was entirely value-driven, with a focus on an enduring purpose
that had little to do with immediate profit. These factors continue
to work today, for example, for Walmart and Mary Kay Cosmetics
in empowering the underdog; Ben & Jerry's and The Body Shop in
social and environmental activism; and Merck, Honda, Sony, and
3M in efforts to produce responsible technological innovations.

Former French president and later president of INSEAD Giscard d'Estaing pointed out that much greater social cohesion will
be achieved if the objective of profit seeking is joined with concern
for contributing to the enduring success of the enterprise and
enriching the life of everyone who participates in it. This consideration has its place in the business strategies of contemporary
companies. The growing number of seminars on the role of corporate management in the United States, Europe, and Japan, and
the spate of best-selling management books on the responsibility
of business enterprises indicate that forward-looking managers are
willing to listen and to act. Doing so is in their own interest: in a
globalized economy only responsible companies can lead—or even
survive.

A CHECKLIST OF RESPONSIBLE MANAGEMENT

RESPONSIBILITY TOWARD SHAREHOLDERS

◆ The company meets shareholder expectations without impairing its social,
physical, or business environment.

◆ Annual reporting is provided to shareholders on legal and regulatory compliance as well as on social and environmental initiatives beyond compliance.

◆ The company's investment strategy has negative selection criteria for activities that involve undesirable social, environmental, and business practices.

◆ The company's investment strategy has positive selection criteria for activities
that involve desirable social, environmental, and business practices.

RESPONSIBILITY TOWARD EMPLOYEES

◆ The company's vision and values are articulate to employees with measurable standards of business ethics, social responsibility, and environmental sustainability.

◆ Employees contribute to the formulation of the company's vision and values at their level and embody them in day-to-day practice.

◆ Annual performance evaluations, compensation systems, and career progression criteria fully integrate the company's vision and values.

◆ The company is actively engaged in the lives of its employees, learning their concerns, understanding their needs, and contributing to their personal development.

RESPONSIBILITY TOWARD CLIENTS AND CUSTOMERS

◆ The company accurately represents its products and services relative to their long-term benefits and costs including safety, social consequences, environmental toxicity, reusability, and recyclability.

◆ The company makes its best effort to educate customers as to the social and environmental desirability of its products and services from cradle-to-grave.

◆ The company's innovation and product development strategy shapes the industry toward greater sustainability, social responsibility, and corporate citizenship.

RESPONSIBILITY TOWARD BUSINESS PARTNERS

◆ The company does not do business with companies that knowingly degrade or otherwise cause significant damage to the environment or behave unfairly toward employees, customers, business partners, or local communities.

◆ The company offers preferential status whenever possible to business partners evidencing ethical leadership.

RESPONSIBILITY TOWARD LOCAL COMMUNITIES

◆ The company does not do business in markets or support regimes that violate basic human rights.

◆ In addition to established corporate giving or patronage programs, the company is actively engaged in the life of its local communities, learning their concerns, understanding their needs, and contributing to their development.

- There is open dialogue between the company and the communities in which it operates.

- Employees of the company are encouraged and given opportunities to devote part of their time to socially responsible activities, doing volunteer work or contributing to the conservation and revitalization of the community.

- The company respects the diversity of the economic, social, cultural, and political conditions in the communities in which it operates.

RESPONSIBILITY TOWARD THE ENVIRONMENT

- The company complies with environmental regulations and laws.

- The company consistently seeks pollution prevention and waste minimization in its supply chain. It anticipates environmental regulation by taking the initiative in reducing negative impacts on the environment.

- The company establishes its own Environmental Management System.

- The company actively pursues eco-efficiency and de-materialization of its value-added to customers.

- The company is continually designing itself for environmental sustainability, including recycling nonrenewable resources, consuming renewable resources at a rate that allows them to regenerate, and limiting the reduction of bio-diversity.

SOURCE: The Club of Budapest, in consultation with the Innov-Ethics Group (IEG), the club's partner in bringing a new ethics to business.

Hardly anybody would contest that in the long term corporate and public interests coincide. Every business needs a satisfied public with buying power, and every public needs the products and services offered by a flourishing industry. But business people are fond of quoting Lord Keynes, who once said that "in the long term we will all be dead." That is true, but today there is an important difference. In a rapidly changing world, time horizons shrink and the long term becomes a matter of only a few years. And in a matter of years we shall not all be dead—but some of us may be out of business. Companies today who fail to care for their stakeholders fail themselves—and tomorrow will themselves fail.

Political Responsibilities

In the critical phase of a macroshift individual responsibilities extend beyond the personal and the business sphere to the civic and political sphere. All spheres of society influence the outcome of the macroshift, and all spheres must shoulder their share of the responsibility for a positive outcome. This means responsibility on the part of the plain citizen. Even if we do not have the privilege of making decisions in politics, in a democracy we can exercise the power of electing and supporting the leaders who do.

The current responsibility of political leaders is by no means negligible. The effective power of governments has been reduced by the rising power of business enterprises, but national governments remain answerable for the welfare of their people, for their freedom, health, and social and environmental security.

If elected leaders are to meet these challenges, they must enlarge their horizons beyond the traditional sphere of political concerns. In the past, the perceptions of national politicians centered on the interests of their own constituencies. But in today's world the interests of local constituencies can no longer be fully represented by policies whose scope is limited to the local or even to the national scene. Governments are not required to interfere in the affairs of other states, but they must join forces with other states and their leaders in tackling the problems and challenges they face in common.

Lifting the sights of national politicians beyond the confines of their own constituencies is not a simple matter. The way most democracies work, national leaders, if they are to stay in power, must confine their attention to the few problems that occupy their electorate's attention. They cannot afford to pay much attention to a host of other issues, even if they are just as important. Action on complex and controversial problems calls for time-consuming public and legislative debate and carries political risks that politicians do not embrace unless they have strong motivation to do so. It is easier and politically more expedient to ignore people who raise issues that do not have the attention of the media and the public, or that lack the backing of influential lobbies and pressure groups, than to champion such politically thankless tasks. In consequence, political action tends to be narrowly focused and neglectful of many of the fundamental issues that shape the contemporary world.

The political process itself selects against commitment to basic and long-term questions. Ballots carry the names of individuals who for the most part have a taste for power and a high level of competitiveness. Those who prefer cooperation to competition, knowledge to power, and are concerned with long-term issues rarely present themselves for election—and even more rarely are they elected to powerful positions. Economist Kenneth Boulding's "dismal theorem" states that most of the skills that lead to the rise of political power make those who possess the skills unfit to exercise that power.

Some political figures show a significant level of commitment to the public good and a genuine wish to serve it. But even when intentions are honorable, actions tend to be less than effective. If politicians become aware of issues that are of fundamental importance but are not in the public eye, they can fund studies, make reports, and hold conferences. Unless they receive public approbation, however, they cannot act. Al Gore observed in his book *Earth in the Balance*, "Ironically, at this stage, the maximum that is politically feasible still falls short of the minimum that is truly effective."

Effectiveness is further reduced by contemporary nation-states being too big to cope with some issues and too small to deal with others. On one hand, decisions that touch people's lives, whether through education, employment, law and order, or civil liberties, require decision-making that is closer to the grassroots than the majority of today's national governments. On the other hand, decision-making in the economic sphere requires a sphere of control and competence larger than that of today's nation-states. Transborder economies of scale are essential for the efficient exploitation and use of natural resources as well as for the optimum employment of labor and the marketing of products and services.

The current scope of national decision-making is too small also in regard to territorial and environmental security. National armies can no more ensure the inviolability of a country's borders than national regulations can safeguard the integrity of its natural environment. Yet the potential for international conflict is growing. Referring to *Global Trends 2015*, the previously cited nonclassified intelligence report, John Gannon, chairman of the U.S. National Intelligence Council noted that, although the risk of war among developed countries will be low, there is growing potential for conflict due to national and regional instability. There is a high potential for ongoing conflict in sub-Saharan Africa, in the Caucasus and Central Asia, in parts of South and Southeast Asia, Central America, and the Andean Region. Rivalries between India and Pakistan and China and Taiwan will not end, nor will the antagonism between Israel and the Arab countries cease. Although the global economy will grow, prosperity will not reach all segments of the population. On the contrary, the information revolution will make the persistence of poverty in the midst of affluence more visible.

As the potential for conflict increases, the lethality of the emerging conflicts will increase as well due to the availability of weapons of mass destruction, longer range missile delivery systems, and similar technologies. But purely military solutions will not work. Gannon suggests that in a world of growing conflict-potential governments will have to broker solutions among a wide array of international actors, including not just other governments but transnational corporations and nongovernmental and nonprofit organizations as well.

THE CASE OF TERRITORIAL AND ENVIRONMENTAL SECURITY

National security in the widest sense calls for a significant level of stability in the international community. However, in today's world security can hardly ever be assured by "sending in the marines." Assuring national security requires wide-ranging cooperation among governments and nongovernmental actors along with adequate military defense capabilities.

If and when defense capabilities are needed, in most cases they can be more effectively mustered by regional defense pacts backed by joint defense forces than by national armies commanded by a single government. In Europe the logic of shifting security from the national to the regional level has been increasingly recognized. It has become evident that persistent conflicts such as those in Kosovo do call for international intervention, but this is best implemented by the region's—in this case the European Union's—peacekeeping forces rather than by powers foreign to the region.

Joint peacekeeping has an economic rationale as well. It frees the participating economies from the burden of maintaining costly armies and enables their governments to use the liberated human and financial resources for productive ends. There is no need to maintain an expensive army if a country can assure its internal and external security with smaller expenditures: the former through a well-equipped police force or national guard, and the latter through a regional peacekeeping force. This logic is becoming accepted in some small and relatively prosperous countries, such as the Nordic and the Benelux countries of Europe, but large states remain reluctant to entrust their national defense to collective peacekeeping. The myth of national sovereignty dictates that territorial security should be ensured by the exercise of national military power.

Environmental security is another area where the scope of governmental action must transcend the borders of the given country. The objectives of environmental protection have been extensively discussed and are widely known. They focus on regulations for mining and using natural resources, on safeguarding the balance and regenerative cycles of nature, and on creation of emergency capacities for dealing with environmental disasters and catastrophes. Implementing these objectives is in every country's vital interest. Every population requires a healthy environment, and every economy needs an assured supply of natural resources.

Yet despite the 1992 Rio Earth Summit, the Kyoto Convention, and other projects and agreements, cooperation in the environmental domain remains underfinanced and mainly on the level of rhetoric. Only half a dozen countries have levied environmental taxes to discourage the unsustainable use of natural resources and energy, and many governments continue to subsidize clear-cutting forests, strip mining, and inefficient uses of water. With the exception of the ozone-destroying CFC reduction convention (encouraged by the availability of economically viable alternatives), only a handful of governments are prepared to bind themselves to specific environmental goals and targets—most governments consider them an infringement on national sovereignty.

While the debates go on and statements of principle are negotiated, few substantive treaties are ratified and even fewer are put into practice. As a result, the stock of nonrenewable resources continues to be depleted, regenerative capacities for a number of renewable resources are further impaired, and the overall livability of the environment is depressed. The statistics speak for themselves. The global emission of carbon from fossil fuels is expected to exceed 1990 levels by 49 percent in the year 2010; forests are disappearing (North and Central America have less than a century of forests remaining, the Caribbean less than fifty years, the Philippines thirty years, Afghanistan sixteen years, and Lebanon fifteen years); a third of the planet's total land surface is threatened with desertification; the atmosphere is heating up; and on average a hundred or more species are lost every day.

Lifting the sights of national politicians above the borders of their country and focusing them on regional and global economic, political, social, and ecological issues is an urgent step whose time has come. The sovereign nation-state is a historical phenomenon: it appeared on the world scene only at the 1648 Peace of Westphalia. In the seventeenth and eighteenth centuries sovereign nation-states spread throughout Europe, and in the twentieth century the wave of decolonization following World War II extended them to all parts of the world. Leaders of the decolonized countries objected to almost everything they inherited from their former colonial masters except the principle of sovereignty. As a result, the world community now consists of nearly two hundred nation-states, including economic giants such as the United States, population giants such as China and India, and a plethora of small and poor states such as Guyana, Benin, and the Seychelles.

Decision-making in a world dominated by nation-states is cumbersome, as seen in the experience of the United Nations. Yet there is nothing in the psychology of citizenship that would forbid the expansion of people's loyalty above the level of the national state. No individual is obliged by his or her emotional make-up to swear exclusive allegiance to one flag only in the conviction that it symbolizes "my country, right or wrong." We can be loyal to several segments of society without being disloyal to any. We can be loyal to our community without giving up loyalty to our province, state, or region. We can be loyal to our region and feel at one with an entire culture and with the human family as a whole. As Europeans are English, Germans, French, Spanish, and Italians as well as Europeans, and as Americans are New Englanders, Texans, Southerners, and Pacific Northwesterners as well as Americans, so people in all parts of the world possess multiple identities and can develop multiple allegiances to go with them.

    It is not reasonable that the attention of governments should remain centered on narrowly focused local issues while business and finance are globalized and the ecological foundations of our lives are threatened. In a complex and interdependent world, effectiveness and efficiency call for widely networked cooperative structures in politics no less than in business.

    A downward transfer of the sovereign powers of national governments is urgent in regard to education, employment, social security, social and economic justice, and local resource use. But an upward transfer is necessary as well in regard to peace and territorial and environmental security in the widest sense, issues that are unmanageable on the local and national levels. In these areas—as well as in finance, communication, and literacy—the rational step is to selectively transfer national sovereignty to jointly constituted regional or global bodies.

    It is not reasonable that the attention of governments should remain centered on narrowly focused local issues while business and finance are globalized and the ecological foundations of our lives are threatened. In a complex and interdependent world, effectiveness and efficiency call for widely networked cooperative structures in politics no less than in business. It is the responsibility of an informed citizenry to elect and support political leaders who are able and willing to enhance their effectiveness by transferring some aspects of national sovereignty downward to local communities and others upward to the international community.

* * * * * * * *

The last but by no means the least of the new imperatives of our time is to accept the multiple facets of the responsibility that falls on our shoulders: As private individuals, we must think globally and act morally. As leaders or collaborators in business, we must care for all stakeholders and for the environment. And as citizens of our country, we must support leaders who recognize the need for locally as well as globally informed and implemented policies.

PART THREE

The Way Ahead

W̶E HAVE ARRIVED AT ONE OF HISTORY'S GREAT WATERSHEDS. The Logos-based civilization of the modern age is not sustainable; it is destined to disappear. Persisting with its values and practices will create deepening rifts between rich and poor, young and old, informed and marginalized, and technological societies and their life-sustaining environment. If we are not to join the myriad species that once populated the Earth but became extinct, we must adapt to the conditions in which we now find ourselves.

We have evolved from Mythos to Theos, and from Theos to Logos. Today, technology or, more exactly, our failure to master technology's side effects and consequences, is pushing us beyond Logos. Attempting to master these side effects with the rational mindset of the modern age is futile. To be sure, we could see further growth in human numbers, in human powers, and in the wealth of a power elite, but we would fail to provide for growth in the quality of life and even for the survival of all the people who inhabit this planet.

The next advance of humankind must be governed by a new rationality. The obsolete and increasingly counterproductive mechanistic rationality of Logos must be replaced by a new holistic rationality of a yet-to-be-born civilization. In the optimum case, this will be a civilization that merits the name *Holos*. Holos civilization is not here yet, but the kind of mindset that could create it is already evolving.

In this concluding section we first consider the kind of development that could shift today's societies from the unsustainable and now strongly counterproductive path of Logos-directed evolution to the more sustainable and humane path of Holos-inspired evolution. Then we review the signs and indications that the consciousness that could empower this shift is here, growing silently but powerfully at the creative margins of society. And last but not least, we address the question that is most crucial of all. Can *you* evolve the new Holos consciousness? For if you can, you can do what few could do before you: You can change the world.

9

Evolution from Logos to Holos

BUSINESS ENTERPRISES, political regimes, local communities, and entire societies envisage the future by looking at the past. The governing assumption is that things will continue in much the same way as before, even if new technologies make some things better, shift the distribution of wealth, and create some areas of conflict. This is today's dominant philosophy about the future: the philosophy of trend extrapolation. It is like driving down a highway by looking at the rearview mirror. As long as the road ahead is reasonably straight, we can steer by the rearview mirror: we just have to make sure that we don't pull too much at the steering wheel. If the road curves, and the curve continues before us, we can still steer by this method. We can even steer by the rearview mirror if the road is getting progressively rocky: we can still hold onto the wheel while making provision for traversing increasingly uneven terrain. But the one condition under which steering by the rearview mirror breaks down is when the road ahead bifurcates. In that case, steering by the road that took us to where we are would lead to a rapid encounter with a ditch.

The road on which humankind now finds itself is not sustainable: it is about to bifurcate. This is the meaning of a macroshift. In its critical chaos phase the system's previous developmental trajectory will give way to a new and different trajectory. In past macroshifts the new trajectory was found—if indeed it was found—by piecemeal trial and error. In a quasi-chaotic situation some things worked out, and others did not. Some societies and civilizations went under, but others survived. Foreseeing the correct path was not entirely critical: the speed by which society approached the bifurcation was relatively modest. Many generations could pass before the correct values, aspirations, beliefs, and behaviors had to crystallize. Today this is not the case. The speed of our collective evolution is unprecedented: we are rushing toward a major bifurcation, and most people do not even know it. It is high time to shift our gaze from the rearview mirror to the landscape ahead.

Another Kind of Evolution

When we behold the landscape in front of us we do not see where we *will* be tomorrow—for that is not decided yet—only where we *could* be. We see that the road ahead forks into many branches. Some are far better than others. There is a branch that leads toward total chaos and anarchy; and another that leads toward a sustainable and humane civilization. There are other branches in-between, but the one branch that does not exist is that which would allow us to move ahead without a change in direction.

Having come to this insight, the question we face is how we should go about changing direction. There is a choice of roads, and this choice, as we have seen, is real. By adjusting our values, aspirations, and behaviors, we can navigate today's macroshift into a new direction. But can we tell into what direction?

> *Logos-inspired evolution was materialistic and conquest- and consumption-oriented. The alternative to it is evolution centered on human development and development of human communities.*

Discovering a feasible direction for our collective evolution is not an insuperable task. It is a direction that departs from twentieth-century Logos-inspired evolution and shifts to a sustainable path. Logos-inspired evolution was materialistic and conquest- and consumption-oriented. The alternative to it is evolution centered on human development and development of human communities. Using simple language, we can say that the now obsolete path was *extensive* evolution, whereas the new and indicated path is *intensive* evolution. Extensive evolution moves along a horizontal plane on the surface of the planet: it conquers ever more territories, colonizes ever more peoples, and imposes the will of the dominant layers on ever more layers of the population. Intensive evolution shifts from the horizontal to the vertical dimension. It reaches to greater heights in the development of mind and consciousness and greater depth in the grounding of community life and intercommunity relations.

The ends and means of intensive evolution are radically different from the ends and means of extensive evolution. A basic end of extensive evolution is the extension of human power over ever-larger areas. Traditionally, the means to this end has been conquest: the conquest of nature and the conquest of other, weaker or less power- and domination-oriented peoples. Successful conquest led to the colonization of nature and of other peoples, to serve the ambitions and interests of the conquerors. For most of recorded history this was accomplished by force of arms. In the twentieth century it was also accomplished through economic means: the power of wealthy states and global companies to impose their will and values on wide layers of the population. For states the goal of extensive evolution was territorial sovereignty, including sovereignty over the human and natural resources of the territories. The corresponding goal for global companies was, and in most cases still is, to generate demand for consumption without much regard for the social and environmental side effects and consequences.

The paramount ends of extensive evolution can be encapsulated in three terms: *conquest*, *colonization*, and *consumption*. They were served by corresponding varieties of technologies. First, the technologies that use and transform matter: the technologies of production. Second, the technologies that generate the power to operate matter-transforming technologies: energy-generating technologies. And third, the technologies that whet people's appetite, create artificial demand, and shift patterns of consumption: the technologies of public relations and advertising.

In the modern age the first of these kinds of technologies built habitations with networks of transportation and communication, and increasingly powerful production structures that yielded a growing variety of products. The second harnessed the forces of nature to drive these technologies. And the third produced the demand-provoking images and the subtle or not-so-subtle means by which the producers of products and services imposed their will on their clients and customers.

In intensive evolution the ends and means are very different. They also can be grasped under three headings: *connection, communication*, and *consciousness*.

Let us take connection first. One of the great myths of the Industrial Age has been the skin-enclosed separation of individuals from each other and from nature and the disjunction of their own interests from the interests of others. The former aspect of this myth has been fueled by classical physics and its success in the domains of engineering. Like the mass points of Newton and the stones, bricks, and other units of mechanical engineering, humans appeared to be self-contained, mutually independent chunks of organized matter only externally related to each other and to their environment. Classical economics reinforced this myth by viewing the individual as a self-centered economic actor, pursuing his or her own interests, harmonized at best with the interests of others through the workings of the market. But today's science has overcome the assumption of separateness. Every quantum is known to be subtly connected with every other quantum in the universe, and every organism with all other organisms in the biosphere. In turn, the contemporary economic system creates a decisive and immediate connection between the interests of individuals, individual states, and individual enterprises, and the workings of the globalized economic system. These embracing connections evolve rapidly, and it is one of the ends of intensive evolution to order them, creating coherent structure in place of random proliferation.

The second aim of intensive evolution is directly linked with the first. It deepens the level of communication and raises the level of consciousness of the communicators. Communication unfolds on multiple levels. First of all, individuals need to communicate with themselves, caring for and developing their inner being. People who are "in touch with themselves" are better balanced and more able to communicate with the world around them. Individuals also need to be better in touch with those who make up the immediate context of their lives—family, community, and work or profession. Still wider levels of communication are equally necessary: communication between people, whether near or far, in their own country or in other countries and cultures, as well as communication with nature, both metaphorically and literally. Intensive evolution means inner-directed development that evolves people's consciousness and helps them find themselves within their social and natural milieu.

Intensive evolution empowers communication between people. Interpersonal communication, as all communication in nature, is made possible by connection, but on the human plane more enters into play than mere connection: communication between humans involves *consciousness*. The full potentials of human communication unfold only when people apprehend the strands of connection through which they communicate. A high level of communication calls for a high level of consciousness to enable the communicators to make use of the many, sometimes extremely subtle, strands of connection that bind them to each other and to nature. Consciousness of these connections is an important factor in our evolution, for it lifts people's thinking and values from an ego-, local community-, and nation-centered orientation to a wider culture- and ultimately species- and planet-centered dimension.

In intensive evolution the overarching aims of connection, communication, and consciousness are served by the selective use of

sophisticated technologies. However, intensive evolution's technologies are different. They ensure connection among humans not
only by the physical exchange of persons and goods, as in extensive
evolution, and not even only by the electronic links created by
information and communication technologies, but also by the
recently rediscovered and in coming decades further developed subtle yet powerful technologies of transpersonal contact and communication. In time electronic information technologies will be
joined by laser-based technologies and by technologies that con-
serve and convey information in the holographic mode.

Given further research and development in the field of energy
technologies, the relatively modest amount of energies required to
operate electronic information technologies will be available on a
sustainable basis by exploiting enduring energy flows rather than
finite and risky energy stocks. In place of fossil and nuclear fuels, the
Sun and processes driven by the energy of the sun can supply the
needed energies. Solar radiation, together with the force of wind
and tide, the fermented by-products of plants and animals, and liquid hydrogen (which can also be generated by the solar catalysis of
sea water) are energy sources several magnitudes larger than any
conceivable human energy demand. In a few decades additional,
though relatively small-scale, energies are likely to become available
by extracting usable energies from the zero-point field of the quantum vacuum. These subtle yet real energies are present throughout
space-time and can also power spacecraft in interplanetary space.

Science will continue to serve human ends as evolution shifts
from the extensive to the intensive path. In addition to energy-flow
and information and communication technologies, science can
refine the technologies for cleaning up the environment and
improving human health. Nanotechnology—using pieces of matter
that vary in size between 0.1 and 100 nanometers (ranging roughly
from the size of atoms to the size of molecules)—can create clean
manufacturing processes by high precision in materials technology,
thus avoiding unwanted and polluting by-products; it can also produce extremely fine filters to remove nanoscale contaminants. It

can further be used to detect toxins and monitor their effects within living cells, a process that may lead to the identification of the correlation between the physiological effects of toxins and environmentally caused diseases. Genetic technology, when responsibly employed, can make use of the knowledge gained in mapping the human genome to eliminate congenital defects and correct some varieties of acquired disease. In time enough information will be available to slow down the aging process and extend the human life span to its natural limits—which may be 120 years, and possibly more.

    ~ Properly pursued, intensive evolution can bring today's macroshift to a soft-landing in a sustainable, globally whole yet locally diverse civilization. ~

In intensive evolution the maintenance of health draws on breakthroughs in genetics and molecular biology as well as on the insights and techniques of holistic medicine. As the growing practice of alternative medicine shows, the organism acts as a whole and, when impaired, can be healed as a whole. Healing the whole organism makes use of the subtle energies that link the human bioenergy field with the fields and radiations of the milieu. Surgical interventions and biochemically based allopathic medications are useful and even essential, but they are therapies of last resort; curative and preventive medicine is best served by bioenergy medicine. Balancing the energy fields of the environment with the bioenergy field of the organism, this new (though in large part only newly rediscovered) form of medicine can strengthen the human immune system and optimize its functioning, averting acute malfunctions.

Properly pursued, intensive evolution can bring today's macroshift to a soft-landing in a sustainable, globally whole yet locally diverse civilization. The likely contours of this possible, but yet-to-be-created holistic world can be envisaged. Envisaging them is a meaningful exercise: it enables us to test our ideas, sharpen the image, and bring it into the range of current hopes and realistic aspirations.

A Holos civilization may sound utopian today, but it could become reality tomorrow. The people who will build it are already born. They are among us and, as we shall see, they are more numerous than we think.

CONTOURS OF THE WORLD AT HOLOS

SOCIAL AND POLITICAL ORGANIZATION

The world at Holos is globally whole but locally diverse. Sovereign nation-states, the inheritance of the modern age, have given way to a transnational world. It is organized as a Chinese box of administrative and decision-making forums, and each forum has its own sphere of authority and responsibility. The new world does not constitute a global hierarchy, for the forums at the different levels have their own autonomy and are not subordinated to the higher levels. Decision-making is global in the areas of trade and finance, information and communication, peace and security, and environmental protection. But the political world is not globally monolithic: it allows and indeed ensures significant autonomy on local and regional levels. Global society constitutes a "heterarchy": a multilevel sequentially integrated structure of distributed decision-making aimed at global coordination combined with regional, national, and local autonomy.

The world community is organized as a sequence of self-reliant communities with multiple links of communication and cooperation. Individuals join together to shape and develop their local community. These communities participate in a wider network of cooperation that includes, but does not cease at, the level of national states. Nation-states are themselves part of regional social and economic communities, coming together in the United Regions organization, the world body resulting from the reform of the United Nations. Its members are not nation-states but the continental and subcontinental economic and social unions that integrate the relevant aspects and shared interests of nation-states. These include the European Union, the North American Union, the Latin American Union, the North-African Middle-Eastern Union, the Sub-Saharan African Union, the Central Asian Union, the South and Southeast Asian Union, and the Australian-Asia-Pacific Union.

The principle of subsidiarity is observed: decisions are made on the lowest level at which they are effective. The global level is the lowest level in regard to ensuring peace and security, and regulating the global flow of goods, money, and knowledge. It is also the level for coordinating the information that flows on globe-spanning channels of communication and harmonizing the policy measures aimed at safeguarding the integrity of the biosphere. The regional level is indicated in turn for decisions that coordinate the social and political aspirations and concerns of nations. The regional economic and social unions provide the forum for elected representatives of member nations to negotiate the interests and aspirations and resolve the problems of their populations. The local level of decision-making consists of the organizations of urban and rural communities. At these forums the representatives of rural zones and urban neighborhoods coordinate their systems of justice and the workings of their social and political institutions in light of the wishes of the people.

LIFESTYLES

People are not all rich, but they all live more simply—simpler than the typical lifestyles of the rich and of those who aspired to be rich in the twentieth century. Simpler lifestyles are not the consequence of rules and legislations or high taxes, although such measures functioned initially as incentives and continue to function as safeguards. They result from the pursuit of a different set of ideals, aimed at leading a healthy life without ostentation, rich in interpersonal contact and contact with nature. The shared aspiration is the development of personality and intellectual and emotional life in the embrace of one's family, community, nation, and region, and in the global community of all peoples, nations, and regions.

People live longer and healthier, but they do not trigger a further growth of the population. They realize that it is irresponsible to produce families beyond the replacement level: two children is the indicated family size in most parts of the globe, except in areas of previously high birth rates where many young people are entering the age of fertility—there one child is the preferred choice. Thus world population is stabilizing at a sustainable level. This has benefits for individuals and families: with modest family size parents are able to better care for their offspring and to ensure that they grow into healthy individuals with sufficient education and access to information to live well and live responsibly.

Life ways are becoming ecologically sustainable. As people are reoriented from conquest and consumption toward developing the structure of personal and social relations and achieving a higher level of personal development, energy and material requirements become more modest and energy and materials use more efficient. Aspirations center less on amassing material goods and more on developing in harmony with nature and communication with each other. Community life enjoys a renaissance—people work together to improve their shared living and working space. There is a renaissance of spirituality as well; women and men are rediscovering a higher dimension of their lives and experience.

Nonetheless, life ways remain socially, culturally, and geographically diverse. Faith, cultural heritage, technological development, level of industrialization, climate, and nature all enter into the choice of lifestyles. Yet all lifestyles have something in common: the valuation of individual and social development with due regard for the advance of human life and civilization on a shared planet.

MORALS

Diversity is joined with unity in the field of morals as well. Moral behavior is assessed in light of the system of values and beliefs of each nation, ethnic group, and community. But beyond the diversity of behavior lies a deeper unity: everyone agrees that it is immoral to live in ways that reduce the chances of life for others. The universal dimension of morality is rooted in a planetary ethic: to live and act in a way that enables others to live as well. To live not necessarily in the same way, but with a real possibility of satisfying basic needs and pursuing a moral path to well-being and fulfillment.

As ethic moves from the margin of holiday sermons and weekend discussions to the center of everyday life, moral considerations enter into the decisions people make in their community and in their business or profession. A planetary ethic enters the political conduct of nations, regions, and the entire human community. It becomes a factor in the management of business enterprises from corner shops to multinational companies.

Following the example of nature as a self-evolving system rather than an arena for life-or-death struggle, the new ethic replaces cut-throat competition with spirited rivalry in the context of shared values and interests. This makes for more conscious and responsible consumer choices, with a preference for products with low material and high information content, and for services that guide and facilitate personal development, bringing an improvement in the quality of life without creating unnecessary increments in the material standard of living.

WORLDVIEW

The view people hold of themselves, of nature and the cosmos is culturally colored and hence locally diverse, but it, too, has an element of unity. The holistic worldview emerges from all spheres and dimensions of experience: from science and from art, from organized religion and from experiential spirituality, and from people's involvement with personal development and from community building. It bolsters and gives direction to the new morality, the new system of social, economic, and political organization, and the search for simpler and more responsible lifestyles.

The holism of the new civilization is not a "metaphysical" or esoteric appendage, or even a radically new discovery—it has been present in all cultures in one form or another for millennia. But in the twenty-first century the natural and the human sciences support society's emerging holism. Physicists know that every quark and every atom is intrinsically linked with every other and that the universe evolves as a whole over the vast expanses of cosmic space and time. Biologists recognize that all of nature constitutes a complex system, feeding on energy from the Sun and cycling it through myriad species, ecosystems, and environments. Social scientists come to the insight that, at their best, human societies, and the global community of all societies, form a complex system that acts as a whole and evolves as a whole, integrating all its peoples and all cultures without negating their identity or canceling their diversity.

At all levels of the vast and complex system in which people participate, self-reliance is the goal and voluntary cooperation the means to achieve it. People recognize their unity within their social and cultural diversity and become conscious architects of their destiny.

IO

The Quiet Dawn of Holos Consciousness

THE OLD TESTAMENT TOLD US, "where there is no vision, the people perish." Today we need the vision to move from economic globalization to a new and sustainable civilization, shifting from the world of modern-age Logos to the postmodern civilization of Holos. For such a shift to occur a new vision and consciousness are essential. In a democracy we cannot change the direction of our collective evolution by political or religious dictates; the insight and the will must come from below, from the people themselves.

Fortunately, a new consciousness is already surfacing at society's creative edge. A quiet but significant groundswell is building today, made up of people who are changing their preferences, priorities, values, and beliefs. The shift is from consumption based on quantity toward selectivity in view of quality defined by environmental friendliness, sustainability, and the ethics of production and use. Lifestyles hallmarked by matter- and energy-wasteful ostentation are changing to modes of living marked by voluntary simplicity and the search for a new morality and harmony with nature.

These changes in values and consciousness, though generally dismissed or underestimated, are both rapid and revolutionary. They are occurring in all segments of society, but most intensely in the emerging cultures where people are dedicated to the search for new patterns of consumption, new lifestyles, and greater responsibility in every aspect of their life.

Numerous grassroots movements and communities are opting out of the mainstream and reforming themselves. These groups are barely visible, since for the most part their members go about their business without trying to convert others or call attention to themselves. They underestimate their own numbers and lack social organization and political cohesion. Yet the more serious and sincere of these cultures merit recognition. Unlike esoteric cultures and sects, members of these cultures do not engage in antisocial activities, indulge in promiscuous sex, or seek isolation. Rather, they try to rethink accepted beliefs, values, and life ways and to strike out on new paths of personal and social behavior to the best of their insights, abilities, and possibilities.

> ∼ *Dismissing or distrusting all people who do not accept the current system of values and the associated worldviews and lifestyles is naïve and indiscriminate. Some alternative cultures may be escapist, introverted, and narcissistic, but the more serious have a genuine core of beliefs that is highly significant in encouraging a positive shift in our consciousness.* ∼

The people who join these groups are united by the aspiration to live a more simple, healthy, natural, and responsible life. They are appalled by what they see as the heartless impersonality and mindless destructiveness of establishment society. The rise of inner-city deprivation and violence, the drift toward anarchy and ethnic intolerance, the impotence of police and military measures to cope with it, the dissolution of the social contract between society and worker, and the rise of unemployment and homelessness prompt ever more people to alter their thinking and their beliefs.

Establishment society seldom differentiates between the more and the less sincere and serious brands of this emerging culture, viewing most groups with mistrust. The labels "esoteric" and "New Age" are frequently applied to these groups, and they are dismissed as marginal or branded as a threat to sanity or law and order. This is unfortunate. Dismissing or distrusting all people who do not accept the current system of values and the associated worldviews and lifestyles is naive and indiscriminate. Some alternative cultures may be escapist, introverted, and narcissistic, but the more serious have a genuine core of beliefs that is highly significant in encouraging a positive shift in our consciousness. To dismiss all emerging cultures indiscriminately is to throw out the baby with the bath water.

The Rise of Spirituality

Perhaps the most promising "baby" of the emerging cultures is spirituality. This need not mean adherence to a formal religion or an organized church; it can also be an inner-directed attitude, a search for personal identity and meaning in life.

> ∼ *Unlike religion, spirituality does not require a particular place for its exercise, nor does it require a priesthood. Its temple is the mind of the individual, and its altar is the state of consciousness that comes about through deep meditation and prayer.* ∼

Spirituality is a private matter, penetrating the relationship between the individual and the cosmos. Unlike religion, spirituality does not require a particular place for its exercise, nor does it require a priesthood. Its temple is the mind of the individual, and its altar is the state of consciousness that comes about through deep meditation and prayer. Its renaissance is not confined to the emerging cultures; concern with spirituality has entered the hallowed halls of higher education. Harvard and other major medical schools are giving courses on spirituality in medicine, and top business schools are offering seminars on spirituality in business. Public-spirited organizations such as the John Templeton Foundation fund research, publications, symposia, and programs that bring together science, medicine, and spirituality. Avant-garde institutions, among them the California Institute of Integral Studies, the Institute of Noetic Sciences, and the Schumacher College of England, devote entire programs to the spiritual tradition and its role in science and society, and some newly founded institutions, such as the Canonbury Masonic Research Centre, are entirely devoted to the study of the mystical tradition, not as historical fact or anthropological curiosity but as a living force of direct relevance to society.

This emerging spirituality is different from traditional religiosity, but it is not opposed to the religious tradition. At their origins all the great religions promoted spirituality among their followers. They were committed to the kind of experience William James described in his seminal work *The Varieties of Religious Experience*. According to James, the hallmark of religious experience is a sense of union with something higher than oneself—a sense that one is part of a deeper, more meaningful reality. The founders of the great religions and their original followers must have had first-hand experiences of this kind. The visions of the Hindu rishis, the Buddha's enlightenment under the Bodhi tree, Mohammed's miraculous journey, Moses' vision of Jehovah in the burning bush, Jesus' temptation by the Devil and communion with God on the cross, Ezechiel's vision of the flaming chariot, and St. John's apocalyptic revelation on Patmos are examples of deep spiritual experiences. The scriptures that followed from them were intended as records and reminders of them.

Regrettably, in the course of time much of the original substance of religious experience has evaporated, leaving some religions and some religious communities with an empty shell of doctrines and rituals. Direct access to a higher reality tends to be reserved for the priests, the appointed mediators between society and the divine. Monks and other members of the ordained priesthood still engage in practices conducive to the religious experience: intense prayer and deep meditation, fasting, silence, and some forms of physical deprivation. But, as Stanislav Grof remarked, if a layperson had a genuine religious experience in one of today's churches, the average priest would probably send him or her to a psychiatrist.

The rise of spirituality in the emerging cultures is independent of the growth of religiosity in society and is not mirrored in church going. Indeed, people who are religious in the classical doctrinaire and church-going sense are often not the people who are deeply spiritual. Just as in the contemporary denominations there is religion with little or no spirituality, in the emerging cultures there is spirituality with little or no religiosity.

Yet a reconciliation between inner-directed spirituality and organized religion is not impossible. In the opinion of visionary theologian Thomas Berry, this requires a new and more adapted view of the world. In *The Dream of the Earth*, and again in *The Universe Story*, Berry suggests that the required view—he calls it the "new story"—comes to us from a reinterpretation of science's world picture. In this reinterpretation the divine is intrinsic to all things, from atoms to galaxies, and the cosmos is our true sacred community. The trends that bring a deeper understanding of ourselves and of our relation to the cosmos are the same trends that shaped the course of the heavens, lighted the sun and formed the Earth, brought forth the continents, the seas, and the atmosphere, awakened life in the primordial cell, and then brought into being the endless variety of living beings.

Berry's spiritual interpretation of the world depicted in natural science is a contemporary variant of the naturalism of St. Francis of Assisi, the evolutionism of Jesuit biologist Pierre Teilhard de Chardin, and the "reverence for life" of missionary doctor Albert Schweitzer. It is fed by the same wellspring of spirituality as the thinking of the great reformers of the past, from Martin Luther to Martin Luther King.

The Renaissance of Civic Programs and Projects

A wide variety of programs and projects inspired and motivated by a growing spirituality are designed and carried out today at the grassroots level. They aim to revitalize the life of the community and to rebuild community itself in a more humane and sustainable form. According to repeated surveys by California's Institute of Noetic Sciences, the current renaissance of community activism includes many programs and projects:

- Programs that foster a spirit of service and provide opportunities for volunteers to contribute to the creation of a better world.

- Policies and programs that facilitate a shift in attitudes and practices concerning crime and war, focusing on legitimated constraint rather than legitimated violence.

- Education programs in groups and organizations concerned with the principles and practices of transformative learning.

- Society-wide programs that discourage mindless consumption and acquisitive materialism, promoting in their place the values of frugality and voluntary simplicity;

- An increasingly rich menu of transformationally oriented programming in socially responsible information and communication media.

- Multiple stakeholder collaborative problem-solving practices in organizations and communities, leading to a growing participation of people in revitalized civil society.

- Promotion of ecologic-economic sustainability by public sector organizations and private sector businesses through policies and processes that bring economic activity into alignment with the principles of natural systems.

- Steps toward agricultural reform and sustainable agricultural practices through the conversion of vast agricultural holdings to family and cooperative farms serving local markets through bio-intensive methods and recycling of organic wastes.

- Innovative partnerships in the public, private, as well as independent sectors to provide opportunities for creative work capable of serving the common good and fostering a sense of purpose.

- Multiple initiatives to change social incentive systems—through taxes, legislation, regulation, subsidies, and the like—oriented toward discouraging excessive resource use and distinguishing between ethical investment and mere speculation.

- Partnerships in the public, private, and independent sectors that support citizens in physically rebuilding their neighborhoods, communities, or cities.

- "Noetic" technologies that foster creativity, promote community building, and nurture a broad range of human potentials.

- Projects to create a new system of indicators to provide comprehensive and forward-looking measures of societal health and well-being.

These programs and projects indicate specific mindset shifts that are hopeful signs within society's general macroshift.

The shift from competition to reconciliation and partnership: a change from relationships, organizational models, and societal strategies based on competition to those based on principles of healing, reconciliation, forgiveness, and professional as well as male-female partnership.

The shift from greed and scarcity to sufficiency and caring: a change in values, perspectives, and approaches from the traditional self-centered and greedy mode toward a sense of the sufficient and the interpersonal concern of caring.

The shift from outer to inner authority: the change from reliance on outer sources of "authority" to inner sources of "knowing."

The shift from separation to wholeness: a fresh recognition of the wholeness and interconnectedness of all aspects of experience and reality.

The shift from mechanistic to living systems: a shift of attention from models of the world, organizations, and human experience based on our acquaintance with mechanistic systems to perspective and approaches rooted in the principles that inform the realms of life.

The shift from organizational fragmentation to coherent integration: a shift from disintegrative, fragmented organizations with parts set against each other so that the fabric is torn and can be manipulated to the advantage of some at the expense of others, to goals and structures so integrated that what people aim for serves both them and all others.

New and more humane and responsible civic projects and programs emerge also under conditions of conflict and deprivation. "Projects around the World," a collection of 487 innovative development projects collected by "Hanover 2000," the German world exposition of the year 2000, includes, besides projects of alternative technology and more efficient resource use, projects and programs inspired by a remarkably adapted civic spirit. For example:

- In Haiti's Port-au-Prince, Radyo Timoun gives a voice to homeless street children: they tell about their own situation, their illtreatment, their needs and fears, and about their hopes for a better world.

- Israel's Givat Haviva Peace Education Center runs two-year courses for Jewish and Arab children to get to know each other and sort out their fears and prejudices. For young people from Israel's areas of ethnic and religious confrontation the Yaari Association's Youth Institute offers seminars to enable them to discover tolerance and develop respect and understanding for their supposed enemies. In turn, the Palestinian authority's Talitha Kumi School organizes intensive encounters with Israeli schoolchildren.

- Some of Nairobi's street children enter the workshops of "Streetwise," where boys paint household articles and the girls sew. They earn a small income that enables them to escape their dependence on the jungle of the streets and attend school.

■ In Sudan the Displaced Women Population and Development Project provides vocational training in sewing, home economics, and soap-making for women refugees of the civil war, while their children are watched and cared for. They also receive small loans to set them up in an activity that could enable them to earn their own living.

■ An innovative theatre group, the Samamu troupe, confronts people in Uganda with stories of corruption, illustrating its destructive effects and showing ways people can resist it. In Mali, another troupe, the Centre Djoliba, uses dance, dramatic sketches, and puppet theater to educate people in the most remote villages about the problems of AIDS, drug abuse, family planning, deforestation, and water shortages.

■ The Barefoot College of Rajasthan in India runs 150 evening schools in 89 villages on the motto that all essential needs can be met with the knowledge and the skills possessed by the villagers. Without the help of outside experts, electricity in the villages is generated with solar energy, and underground water tanks are dug to provide people, animals, and plants with a dependable source of water.

■ Colombia's FUNDAEC (Fundacion para la Aplicacion y Enseñanza de las Ciencias) equips young people from rural areas with the skills they need to live in the countryside, helping to stem their migration toward the cities.

■ The Grameen Bank of Bangladesh, a pioneer of the practice of "microcredits," gives villagers, mostly women, small loans to buy a cow, set up a shop, or engage in some other remunerative activity. The borrowers develop business ideas in small groups and the responsibility for repayment is borne by the group as a whole. In a related endeavor Kolping India enables villages in Tamil Nadu to set up savings associations. Groups of villagers pay a small amount into a savings account from which they obtain interest-free loans to finance their own projects.

- In India's desert region of Rajfasthan, the nongovernmental Lokhit Pashu-Palak Sansthan organization enables the Raika camel herdsmen to sustain themselves by supplementing their traditional veterinary knowledge with modern medicines and helping them market the milk of their camels.

- Likewise in India, women from the region of Madras launched their own Working Women's Co-operative Society. Since its founding in 1981 the society has grown into the nationwide Indian Co-operative Network for Women. With small credits women start their own businesses or repair their houses and escape from perpetual debt to moncylenders.

- In Guinea-Bissau an association of blacksmiths (AFGB, Assosiação dos Ferreiros da Guiné-Bissau) helps local artisans rediscover and develop traditional blacksmith techniques, replacing expensive plastic utensils with environment-friendly iron products and creating new jobs.

- And, in perhaps the most dramatic civic project of all, 4,000 families of the "Payatas Waste Pickers," traditionally picking the slums of the Philippines, are joined together in a rubbish-collection project that both provides them with a livelihood and contributes to cleaning up the worst of Manila's slums.

Emerging Cultures in the United States

In the United States, at the center of the industrialized world, a new consciousness is rapidly emerging. This is the surprising conclusion of a series of opinion surveys carried out by public opinion and market researcher Paul Ray. In surveys conducted periodically throughout the 1990s, he found that a particular variety of alternative culture is growing rapidly. This culture, identified as the "cultural creatives," is ignored by the mainstream and underestimated by the members of the culture themselves.

The cultural creatives are one of two major alternative cultures in the United States; the other is the culture of the "traditionals," people who opt out of the mainstream by harking back to the seemingly ideal conditions of bygone times. By contrast, the cultural creatives divorce themselves from the establishment by endeavoring to evolve their values and vision and change their lifestyle.

The mainstream of the U.S. population from which the creatives and the traditionals wish to differentiate themselves is the culture of the "moderns." The moderns, the traditionals, and the cultural creatives each have their specific values, beliefs, and lifestyles. The moderns are stalwart supporters of consumer society. They share the Logos rationality that shaped it and brought U.S. society to dominance today. Their culture is that of the office towers and factories of big business and of the banks and stock markets. Its values are taught in most prestigious schools and colleges in the United States. In 1999 this was the culture of some 48 percent of the American people: 93 million out of about 193 million adults, more men than women. Family income was $40,000 to $50,000 per year, situating moderns in the middle to upper income bracket.

The traditionals made up 24.5 percent of the U.S. population in 1999: 48 million adults. They come from a variety of socioeconomic and ethnic backgrounds, with family incomes in the relatively low range of $20,000 to $30,000 per year, due among other things to the diminished income of the many retirees among them. Demographically, traditionals are both older and less educated than the other two U.S. population segments. More than two-thirds are religious conservatives who oppose abortion, but beyond that there is hardly any political and strategic consensus among them.

The other U.S. alternative culture movement, that of the cultural creatives, consists of more women than men. Its total share is 23.4 percent of the adult population of the United States, and their members range from the middle classes to the wealthy class. The factor that identifies them is less what they preach than what they practice, for cultural creatives seldom attempt to convert others, preferring to be concerned with their own personal growth. Their behavior, especially their lifestyle choices, differentiate them from the other cultures.

THREE KINDS OF AMERICAN VALUES AND LIFESTYLES

MODERNS

Moderns share many of the positive virtues and values typical of the U.S. population: being honest, the importance of family and education, belief in God, and a fair day's pay for a fair day's work. But they also have values and beliefs that distinguish them from the major alternative U.S. cultures. These include:

◆ Making or having a lot of money

◆ Climbing the ladder of success with measurable steps toward one's goals

◆ "Looking good" or being stylish

◆ Being on top of the latest trends and innovations

◆ Being entertained by the media

For the most part, moderns believe that

◆ the body is much like a machine.

◆ organizations, too, are very much like machines.

◆ either big business or big government is in control and knows best.

◆ bigger is better.

◆ what can be measured is what gets done.

◆ analyzing things into their parts is the best way to solve a problem.

◆ efficiency and speed are the top priorities—time is money.

◆ life can be compartmentalized into separate spheres: work, family, socializing, making love, education, politics, and religion.

Being concerned with spirituality and the inner dimensions of life, moderns believe, is "flaky" and immaterial to the real business of living.

TRADITIONALS

Traditionals opt out of the mainstream by looking to the values and lifestyles they believe characterized the American scene in the past. For example:

◆ Patriarchs should again dominate family life.

◆ "Feminism" is a swearword: men need to keep to their traditional roles, and women to theirs.

◆ Men should be proud to serve their country in the military.

◆ Freedom to carry arms is essential for everyone.

◆ Family, church, and community is where everybody belongs.

◆ The conservative version of whichever religion one belongs to is the correct one.

◆ All the guidance one needs in life can be found in the Bible.

◆ Customary and familiar ways of life should be maintained.

◆ Rural and small town life is more virtuous than big city and suburban life.

◆ Sex should be regulated, including pornography, teen sex, and extramarital sex.

◆ Abortion is a sin against life.

◆ The country should do more to support virtuous behavior.

◆ Restricting and punishing immoral behavior is more important than assuring civil liberties.

◆ Foreigners and foreign things are an unwelcome presence.

Traditionals are outraged about the disappearance of the small town way of life they claim to remember and now hark back to. Some among them take the small town Main Street business stance against big business Wall Street ethics; others harbor the traditional working-class resentment of big and wealthy corporations.

CULTURAL CREATIVES

The hallmark of the other alternative culture movement, the cultural creatives (CCs), is an entire repertory of changed behaviors and lifestyle choices:

Books and radio: CCs buy more books and magazines and listen to more radio, preferably news and classical music, and watch less television than any other group.

Arts and culture: Many CCs are aggressive consumers of the arts and culture; they are likely to go out and get involved, whether as amateurs or as professionals.

"Whole process" information: CCs want the "whole process" story of whatever they get in their hands, from cereal boxes to product descriptions to magazine articles. They dislike superficial advertising and product description, wanting to know how things originated, how they were made, who made them, and what will happen to them when they are discarded.

Authenticity: CCs want real, "authentic" goods and services. They have led the consumer rebellion against products considered fake, imitation, throwaway, cliché, or merely fashionable.

Selective consumption: CCs do not buy on impulse but research what they consume, reading labels and assuring themselves that they are getting what they want. Many are typical consumers of the "experience industry" that offers intense, enlightening, or enlivening experience rather than a specific product (weekend workshops, spiritual gatherings, personal growth experiences, experiential vacations, and so on). With regard to nonexperiential products, they prefer ecologically sound, efficient goods to mere style and comfort (for instance, ecologically sound high-mileage recyclable cars with top customer service).

Soft innovation: CCs do not simply buy the latest gadgets and innovations on the market; many creatives are just getting onto the Internet. They tend to be innovators and opinion leaders for knowledge-intensive products, including magazines, fine foods, and selected wines and beverages.

Eating habits: The creatives are "foodies"; they like to talk about food, experiment with new kinds of food, eat out, or cook with friends, trying gourmet, ethnic, and natural health foods.

Home styles: CCs buy fewer new houses than people of their income level in other groups because they view the available housing unsuited to their lifestyle. Instead, they mostly buy resale houses and fix them up to their liking. They avoid status displays with impressive columns and entrances, preferring inward-looking spaces hidden by fences and shrubbery. They want their home to be a "nest," with many interesting nooks and niches. CCs like to work at home and often convert a bedroom or den into a home-office.

Holism: The common thread among CCs is their holism. This comes to the fore in their preference for natural whole foods, holistic health care, holistic inner experience, whole system information, and holistic balance between work and play and consumption and inner growth. They view themselves as synthesizers and healers, not just on the personal level but also on the community and the national levels, even on the planetary level. They aspire to create change in personal values and public behaviors that could shift the dominant culture beyond the fragmented and mechanistic world of the moderns.

SOURCE: Paul H. Ray and Sherry Ruth Anderson, *The Cultural Creatives*. Harmony Books, New York, 2000.

The relative growth of the mainstream and of the two alternative cultures is highly significant. Moderns still constitute the most populous and stable segment and traditionalist culture is shrinking. As older members die, they are not being replaced by nearly as many younger people. In the mid-1990s, 50 percent of Americans were traditionals, but today there are fewer than 25 percent, with projections showing continued decline. In contrast, the cultural creative population is growing. The segment of cultural creatives in the U.S. population consisted of five million adults in 1965; even twenty years ago its share was less than 3 percent of the total. Today cultural creatives total nearly fifty million people—and their numbers are growing rapidly.

These trends are not generally known, even by those who are responsible for them. Moderns firmly believe they are the representative majority and will remain so. Traditionals claim that they are the winners of the "culture war" with the moderns, citing as evidence the proliferation of conservative radios stations and the swelling membership of some megachurches and conservative denominations. And cultural creatives continue to underestimate their own numbers. Many believe this group constitutes no more than 5 percent, or maximum 10 percent, of the adult U.S. population—far from their actual 23.4 percent share.

Because the cultural creatives do not know their own share in American life, they underestimate the potential weight of their movement. They are culturally and politically weak beyond their numbers, lacking social cohesion and an organized basis for supporting each other. In consequence they are underestimated by big business and the media, and ignored by the majority of politicians. This situation is not very different in other parts of the world. "Voluntary simplicity in lifestyles" was one of the top ten trends of the year 1997 according to the Trends Research Institute of New York, spreading to Europe, Australia, and Canada. The Institute found that masses of people are beginning to embrace the belief that they can enhance the quality of their lives by cutting back on the quantity of the products they consume. The same year a survey by the European Union's monthly Euro-Barometer queried people in all fifteen of the Union's member states as to their cultural and lifestyle preferences. It appears that cultures similar to the cultural creatives are present in Europe, in much the same proportions as in the United States. Yet they are hardly better known or more influential than their American counterparts.

Duane Elgin of the San Anselmo Indicators Project reviewed the goals and behaviors of a variety of emerging cultures in the United States and abroad. He found that they are bridging differences, harmonizing efforts, connecting people and helping them discover higher common ground. Their shared objectives are to nurture global ecological awareness, evolve better values, create more sustainable patterns of living, evolve globe-spanning communication systems, and achieve spirituality through personal experience. Elgin concluded that a new global culture and consciousness have taken root, a shift in consciousness as distinct and momentous as that which occurred in the transition from the Agricultural to the Industrial Age.

11

You Can Change the World

MARGARET MEAD TOLD US "never to doubt the power of a small group of people to change the world. Nothing else ever has." Mahatma Gandhi was even more insistent: "Be the change you want to see in the world." They were right. When you change yourself, you change the world around you—and ultimately you change the world.

In a macroshift, this insight is crucial. It bears repeating that if the critical chaos phase of this shift is to be brought to a humane and sustainable conclusion, our values, worldviews, ethics, and ambitions must change in line with our changing conditions. We must forget obsolete beliefs, learn to live with and make productive use of the world's persistent diversity, embrace a planetary ethic capable of guiding behavior that can enable all people to live on this Earth, and meet the responsibilities that fall to every one of us in the personal, business, and political spheres of our lives. Understanding these imperatives is essential, but if it remains on the level of the intellect, it is insufficient. A global survey of young people has shown that intellectual understanding produces better ideas, but not necessarily better behaviors.

Designed and implemented by UNESCO and the U.N. Environment Programme, the "Survey on Youth and Sustainable Consumption" interviewed young people in 24 countries on five continents. It found that the vast majority of young people rank the reduction of pollution in air, water, and soil as the most important challenge for their future—more important even than issues of health, human rights, population increase, and the disparity between rich and poor. Yet the survey also found that there is a serious disjunction between the ideals and hopes of youth and their everyday life. Young people in both industralized and developing countries recognize the environmental and social impact of the way they consume and discard the products available to them, yet they do not link this intellectual recognition to the way they shop. Especially when it comes to everyday items such as food and clothing, considerations of price and quality continue to outweigh the environmental friendliness of the products and the social implications of their production and use.

Young people, and people of all ages and all walks of life, can change the world, but only if they go beyond mere understanding and evolve their consciousness. They will then not only *think* better but will also *act* on their thinking—as the U.S. "cultural creatives" already do.

Harry Truman once remarked, "the buck stops here," meaning the desk of the president of the United States. Today the buck has become more democratic: it stops with every one of us, whether rich or poor, developed or developing. It comes in the form of a challenge: Reexamine your values, evolve your consciousness. If you do, the movement toward a more adapted and sustainable civilization will deepen and spread.

Why is your consciousness so crucial? The explanation is common sense, and it makes uncommon good sense. We know that when a living species is threatened with extinction it faces a stark choice: it either produces a viable mutation or becomes extinct. For the species to survive, the way its members maintain themselves and the environment and the way they reproduce have to change. In nonhuman species most behavior directly concerned with survival is genetically coded, and this kind of change calls for a coinciding adaptive mutation of the gene pool.

The situation is not quite the same when it comes to humans. When the survival of a human population is threatened, it too must produce a viable change in the way it lives and reproduces if it is not to face the specter of extinction. But this does not require a mutation of the genetic pool of our species. Although it is true that some aspects of human behavior are genetically coded, the values and beliefs that threaten human survival today are under conscious, not genetic, control. We can discard obsolete beliefs and outdated behaviors and adopt new beliefs and behaviors. This process of "cultural mutation" is far more rapid and efficient than a mutation of the gene pool, which is a protracted process involving repeated trial and error, with the successive mutants exposed to the ultimate test of fitness to the environment—the test of natural selection. The mutation of the cultural information pool does not require the chance serendipity of success: it can be consciously planned and purposively promoted. Its conscious planning and purposive promotion have become a precondition of human survival in the twenty-first century.

A general definition of culture is the ensemble of values, worldviews, aspirations, and customs that characterize a people and distinguish it from others. In this sense there are thousands of cultures in today's world. Yet, with the exception of the few remaining traditional cultures, they all share a common trait: they give rise to behaviors that are socially and ecologically unsustainable. This trait must now disappear—and its disappearance, like any other specific of human culture, hinges crucially on people's consciousness. If the consciousness of mainstream culture does not change, the threat to human survival will persist. Obsolete values and outdated beliefs will widen the gap between rich and poor and degrade the viability of nature. This will lead to deepening social, economic, and political crises, spreading destitution, increasing violence, and ultimately a collapse of the weakest populations.

The threat to human survival has its ultimate roots in the outdated consciousness of a critical mass in today's world. If the obsolescence of today's dominant consciousness is the root cause of the survival threat, evolution of this consciousness is the way to overcome that threat. You, as everyone around you, can do your part by evolving your own consciousness.

⌇ To live with and not against each other, to live in a way that does not rob the chances of others to live as well, to care what is happening to the poor and the powerless as well as to nature calls for feeling and intuition; for sensing the situation in which we find ourselves, apprehending its manifold aspects and creatively responding to it. ⌇

But just how can you evolve your consciousness? First of all, you should know what is a more evolved consciousness. The simplest way to grasp it is in reference to the two frontal hemispheres of your brain, the narrowly rational one-thing-at-a-time rationality of the left hemisphere, and the intuitive, Gestalt-perceiving right hemisphere. The mythical rationality of ages past was right-brain dominated, while the rationality of the modern age is left-brain dominated—it is the rationality of Logos. A more evolved consciousness combines the clear-cut if simplifying linear reasoning of the left-brain with the spontaneous, deep intuitions of the right. It is whole-brain consciousness: the consciousness of Holos.

Having whole-brain Holos consciousness is not a matter of adding more facts and figures to the storehouse of facts and figures already in your head. Relevant facts and figures are important, but alone they do not fill the bill. To live with and not against each other, to live in a way that does not rob the chances of others to live as well, to care what is happening to the poor and the powerless as well as to nature calls for more than reading up on the statistics. It also calls for feeling and intuition, for sensing the situation in which we find ourselves, and for apprehending its manifold aspects and creatively responding to it. It means raising the full scope of our attention, empathy, and concern from today's ego-, business-, and nation-centered dimension to a broader human-, nature-, and planet-centered one.

A more evolved consciousness is achievable; many people are achieving it already. The principal avenues that lead to it are open to everyone.

The Avenue of Inner Experience

⁓ People who meditate or pray, who have had near-death experiences, and who have traveled in space have a fresh appreciation of existence and reverence for nature. . . . They possess an integrated, holistic vision of themselves, of nature, and of the universe. ⁓

Psychiatrists and consciousness researchers know that a more balanced consciousness arises in those who have had direct inner experience of oneness with other people, and with nature. Individuals practicing a deep meditative or prayerful state intuit oneness with other persons or with a higher presence, and those who have come close to death in an accident or illness experience life in a new light. Common characteristics of this inner peace include no fear of death, empathy with other people, and taking pleasure in simple living and sharing. Astronauts who have had the privilege of traveling in space and viewing the Earth in all its living splendor feel an intense tie to their home planet for the rest of their days.

People who meditate or pray, those who have had near-death experiences, and those who have traveled in space have a fresh appreciation of existence and a reverence for nature. They evolve deep humanitarian and ecological concerns and find differences among people, whether in the area of sex, race, color, language, political conviction, or religious belief, interesting and enriching rather than threatening. They realize that they cannot do anything to nature without simultaneously doing it to themselves and that other people—whether next door, in distant parts of the world or of generations yet to come—are not separate from them and that their fate is not a matter of indifference. These people possess an integrated, holistic vision of themselves, of nature, and of the universe.

Not everyone can be expected to engage in deep prayer or meditation, have near-death experiences, or be shot into space—yet a more evolved consciousness is needed in *all* people. Psychiatrist Stanislav Grof believes that this can be achieved: the states of consciousness required for it were common in times past, and can become common again in the future. In ancient and traditional cultures people regularly experienced nonordinary states of consciousness fostered by their socially sanctioned rituals. "Primitive" and traditional people could and very likely did have firsthand experience of deep connections to each other and to all of nature. Shamans and medicine men seem also to have had encounters with archetypal beings and to have entered mythological realms. Not surprisingly, these cultures integrated people's altered-state experiences into their overall worldview.

According to Grof, the same thing is happening to contemporary people who have the opportunity to enter nonordinary states of consciousness. He has yet to meet a single person from our culture, he said, no matter what his or her educational background, IQ, and specific training, who had powerful transpersonal experiences yet continued to subscribe to the materialistic concepts that dominated the mindset of the twentieth century. Even highly trained psychologists, when they have experiences of nonordinary states or study them in others, shift to a vision of the world that integrates the dominant view of modern-age Logos with deeper cultural and historical perspectives. It is likely that if nonordinary states were to become generally accessible, today's dominant consciousness would shift to a new and more adapted modality.

The Avenue through Art

~ *Genuine works of art and literature socialize people into their community and give insight into the relations that bind them to each other and to the cosmos. They give perceptible form to humankind's perennial intuitions of the oneness of life and nature.* ~

Nonordinary states attained through meditation, spirituality, or psychotherapy are not the only avenue leading to an evolution of consciousness. This evolution is a cultural process, and art and artists have an important role in it. Art and literature in their many forms are vital resources for the evolution of new values and perceptions. Despite their specific modes of expression and criteria of excellence, art and literature are nourished by the same basic source as science, philosophy, and spirituality: insight into the nature of human experience. Rather than penetrating the microcosmos of the atom or the macrocosmos of interstellar space, the artist and the writer penetrate the deepest regions of their own psyche to find communal links with their fellow women and men, with their suffering and joy, ambitions and yearnings.

Art is not limited to museums, galleries, and concert halls but is present throughout society. It shapes cities through architecture and urban design, enters people's feelings through music, entertains, challenges, and informs through film, radio and television, and catalyzes comprehension through literature and drama. It is cultural creativity in its finest form.

Genuine works of art and literature socialize people into their community and give insight into the relations that bind them to each other and to the cosmos. They give perceptible form to humankind's perennial intuitions of the oneness of life and nature. They are a vital source of inspiration for living, loving, and harmony with all of creation.

Art is more relevant to the outcome of today's macroshift than most artists and art lovers realize. It is all the more regrettable that artists are often reluctant to go beyond their coterie of experts and followers to address everyone in society—they fear that by so doing they will become propagandizers of preconceived ideologies. Yet by turning to all people with art that expresses their own experience they become propagators of their own consciousness. Great art is not any the less great for addressing the bulk of humankind; it is only more effective in promoting the common good.

The Avenue through Science

⌒ A better grasp of the worldview suggested by the latest scientific theories would give a positive impetus to the evolution of people's consciousness and would move us nearer to a more adapted path for our collective evolution. ⌒

Science is changing. This change, much like the emerging cultures' change of consciousness, is important, yet it is not widely known. Innovations in science—insofar as they do not have immediate technological and economic implications—are poorly communicated to society at large. Scientists use esoteric language and complex mathematics; their reports are neither accessible nor understandable beyond their narrow specialties. The result is that the general public is poorly informed about advances at the cutting edge of scientific thought.

A few scientists have formulated scientific findings in narrative form, using everyday language. Stephen Hawking, Paul Davies, and other scientists produced writings of this sort, and they met with success. Some of their books have become bestsellers. Indeed, the emerging insights are fascinating and can be effectively communicated in many venues—for example, as illustrated accounts of the evolution of the cosmos, life, and consciousness for children; as textbooks on the scientific worldview for students in elementary and middle schools; as reference works on the new sciences in colleges and universities; and as information briefs on the nature and dynamics of social and ecological developments for business leaders and politicians. Television documentaries and the Internet could bring the new scientific worldview to the general public.

The remarkable but as yet little known fact—outlined here in the Postscript—is that science is evolving a holistic way of thinking about the world. This is of direct relevance to navigating the macroshift. A better grasp of the worldview suggested by the latest scientific theories would give a positive impetus to the evolution of people's consciousness and would move us nearer to a more adapted path for our collective evolution. The popular ideas of Newton, Darwin, and Freud have been overtaken by new discoveries. In light of these emerging scientific insights, the universe is no longer seen as a lifeless, soulless aggregate of inert chunks of matter. Rather, it resembles a living organism. Life is not a random accident, and the basic drives of the human psyche include far more than the drive for sex and self-gratification.

In the emerging vision of science, matter, life, and mind are consistent elements within an overall process of great complexity yet coherent and harmonious design. Space and time are united as the dynamic background of the observable universe. Matter is vanishing as a fundamental feature of reality, retreating before energy; and continuous fields are replacing discrete particles as the basic elements of an energy-bathed universe. The universe is a seamless whole, evolving over eons of cosmic time and producing conditions where life, and then mind, can emerge.

Life is an intimate web of relations that evolves in its own right, interfacing and integrating its myriad diverse elements. The biosphere is born within the womb of the universe, and mind and consciousness are born in the womb of the biosphere. Nothing is independent of any other thing. Our body is part of the biosphere, and it resonates with the web of life on this planet. Our mind is part of our body, and it is in touch with other minds as well as with the biosphere.

Inner experience, art and literature, as well as acquaintance with the current discoveries of science are among the many ways that today's cultural mutation could be fostered. Education, both formal and informal, offers additional ways. School and family could encourage children to treasure feelings and empathies that link them to other people, to humanity and to nature. In young people, as well as throughout life, intuitions that give credence and substance to links and bonds with people and nature could be brought to the level of consciousness instead of being suppressed by a modern rationality that ascribes such notions to childish fantasy, if not to an unhinged mind.

Addressing a joint session of Congress in Washington in February of 1991, Czech writer-president Václav Havel said, "Without a global revolution in the sphere of human consciousness, nothing will change for the better . . . and the catastrophe towards which this world is headed—the ecological, social, demographic, or general breakdown of civilization—will be unavoidable." Havel's point was well taken, but it is not a reason for pessimism. The breakdown of civilization can be avoided. Human consciousness can evolve. In a significant number of people it is evolving already. Today's stream of Holos consciousness can swell into a mighty tide that will change the world.

TEN BENCHMARKS OF HOLOS CONSCIOUSNESS

You have whole-brain Holos consciousness when you:

1. Live in ways that enable all other people to live as well, satisfying your needs without detracting from the chances of other people to satisfy theirs.

2. Live in ways that respect the right to life and to economic and cultural development of all people, wherever they live and whatever their ethnic origin, sex, citizenship, station in life, and belief system.

3. Live in ways that safeguard the intrinsic right to life and to a life-supportive environment of all the things that live and grow on Earth.

4. Pursue happiness, freedom, and personal fulfillment in harmony with the integrity of nature and with consideration for the similar pursuits of others in society.

5. Require that your government relate to other nations and peoples peacefully and in a spirit of cooperation, recognizing the legitimate aspirations for a better life and a healthy environment of all the people in the human family.

6. Require business enterprises to accept responsibility for all their stakeholders as well as for the sustainability of their environment, demanding that they produce goods and offer services that satisfy legitimate demand without impairing nature and reducing the opportunities of local enterprises and developing economies to compete in the marketplace.

7. Require public media to provide a constant stream of reliable information on basic trends and crucial processes to enable citizens and consumers to reach informed decisions on issues that affect their health, prosperity, and future.

8. Make room in your life to help those less privileged than yourself to live a life of dignity, free from the struggles and humiliations of abject poverty.

9. Work with like-minded people to preserve or restore the essential balance of the environment, whether in your neighborhood, your country or region, or throughout the world.

10. Encourage young people, and open-minded people of all ages, to evolve the spirit that could empower them to make ethical decisions of their own on issues that decide their future and the future of their children.

Twelve Comments by Members
of the Club of Budapest

Peter Russell . . . on the roots of the global crisis

As Ervin Laszlo makes clear, the global crisis we are now facing is, at its root, a crisis of consciousness. Certainly we need to do everything in our power to curb population growth and reduce the impact our technology has on the planet's ecosystems. But we also need to ask why it is that one species out of millions—a species that considers itself the most intelligent species on this planet—can behave in ways that are clearly not in its long-term self-interest? To realize that we are threatening our own survival, and that of many other species, and then to continue with the very activities that are causing the problem, is nothing short of insane.

The root of the problem lies in our thinking, our attitudes, and our values. We are stuck in an outdated mindset that tells us that if we are to be at peace we need to have the right things. Such an attitude may be important when individual survival is at stake; we need then to focus our attention on our physical well-being. But this is not an issue for most people in the developed world. The world has changed beyond all recognition from preindustrial times, and most of our survival needs are now met. But because we have not changed our thinking, we continue to consume and despoil the planet in the vain hope that if only we had enough of the right things we would find fulfillment. Today it is our collective survival that is at stake—and it is our inner, spiritual well-being that most urgently needs our care and attention.

This is the challenge of the early twenty-first century: exploration of inner space—the development of human consciousness to match the fantastic strides we have made in our material development.

Edgar Mitchell . . . on the challenge, and the vision of science

As one of those who has had the privilege of observing this magnificent little planet from the darkness of space, I join my colleagues of the Club of Budapest who call for a new vision for the future and a new dedication to the proper stewardship of our planet.

From above the protective canopy of our atmosphere one can observe the progressive degradation of the ecological systems upon which all species depend for sustenance. It is clear from that view and with data from four decades of space activity that our burgeoning population has set a course that is not sustainable. We are a species that is incessantly in conflict over mundane issues while ignoring the chasm that lies ahead for us all. We argue from the point of view of our traditional cultural values, unwilling to look at ourselves from the larger global perspective and to take the necessary steps to create a more tranquil and harmonious civilization for our mutual benefit—steps that include some hard choices about our lifestyles.

A significant number of concepts have been advanced by scientists within the past two decades that, when taken together and applied to the metaproblem envisaged through general evolution and systems theory, provide a radically new understanding of the human condition and our place in the cosmos. I refer to experiments in quantum physics that demonstrate "nonlocality" (meaning interconnectedness) at the level of subatomic particles; "quantum holography," which extends that idea to macroscale objects; and work in chaos theory, which suggests the repetition of basic structures across scale sizes from the microscopic to the cosmic. In addition, chaos theory and the theory of complex systems suggest the presence of simple feedback loops that organize the basic structures and processes of nature into the exquisite shapes we find in living matter. I refer to the work of the astronomers and cosmologists who continue to discover the marvels of distant worlds and to the work of Ilya Prigogine, who has shown that nonlinear processes are the most fundamental ones in nature, not the simple, linear, reversible processes that scientists have studied since Newton's time.

The effect of all this is the view that we live in a self-organizing, creative, intelligent, learning, trial-and-error universe that has evolved to "know" itself and has likely spawned intelligent life throughout its expanse. Virtually all the numinous events reported by the esoteric core in every cultural tradition—events that serve as the basis for traditional religious lore—now can be understood in terms that should satisfy the most critical science. The lessons from this view for our times pertain to our evolution as creative, inter-connected, and responsible humans with the fate of our world and all its species resting in our collective hands—dependent upon our vision and wisdom to chart a sustainable course into the future.

We have the knowledge, the wisdom, and the visionaries among us to enable us to understand today's critical issues. We must now find the collective political will to implement and accelerate the necessary steps on a global basis—or suffer the consequences.

Karan Singh . . . on the evolution of the new consciousness

We live in a shrinking world in which the malign heritage of con-flict and competition, and the growing gap between the developed and the developing world, will have to make way for a new culture of convergence and cooperation if the rich promise of the new mil-lennium is not to dissolve into conflict and chaos.

Unprecedented human interventions in the environment have upset the delicate ecological balance that enabled Mother Earth—Bhavani Vasundhara in the Indian tradition, Gaia in the Greek—to survive for billions of years and become a unique crucible for the evolution of consciousness. Ruthless exploitation of nonrenewable natural resources has created havoc and, if allowed to continue, could result in a series of major ecological disasters that would dis-rupt life on this planet in the twenty-first century.

We do not lack the intellectual or economic resources to tackle the problems. Scientific breakthroughs and technological ingenuity have given us the capacity to overcome all challenges. What is missing is the wisdom and compassion to do so. Knowledge proliferates, but wisdom languishes. This yawning chasm needs to be bridged before the end of this decade if we are ever to reverse the present trend toward disaster.

The astounding communications system encircling the globe today seldom uses its tremendous potential to spread global values and foster a more caring, compassionate consciousness. To the contrary, the media is full of violence and horror, cruelty and carnage, unbridled consumerism and unabashed promiscuity, which not only distorts the awareness of the young but dulls our sensitivity to the problems of human suffering and pain. What is urgently needed, therefore, is a U-turn in our educational and communications policies. We need to develop carefully structured programs on a global scale based clearly and unequivocally on the premise that human survival involves the growth of a creative and compassionate planetary consciousness. The spiritual dimension must once again be given importance in our thinking, and for this we must draw upon the great reservoir of idealism and spiritual values provided by the rich religious traditions of humanity.

We need the courage to think globally, to break away from traditional paradigms, and to plunge boldly into the future. We must so mobilize our inner and outer resources that we can consciously build a new world in the twenty-first century based on mutually assured welfare rather than mutually assured destruction.

As global citizens committed to human survival and welfare, we must structure a worldwide program of education—for children and adults alike—that would open their eyes to the reality of the dawning global age and their hearts to the cries of the oppressed and the suffering. There is no time to be lost, because, along with the emergence of global society, the sinister forces of fundamentalism and fanaticism, of exploitation and intimidation, are active as well.

Let us, then, with utmost speed, pioneer and propagate a new, holistic consciousness based upon the following premises:

1. That the planet we inhabit and of which we are all citizens— Planet Earth—is a single, living, pulsating entity; that the human race in the final analysis is an interlocking, extended family— Vasudhaiva Kutumbakam as the Veda has it; and that differences of race and religion, nationality and ideology, sex and sexual preference, economic and social status—though significant in themselves—must be viewed in the broader context of global unity.

2. That the ecology of Planet Earth has to be preserved from mindless destruction and ruthless exploitation and enriched for the welfare of generations yet unborn; and that there must be a more equitable consumption pattern based on limits to growth, not unbridled consumerism.

3. That hatred and bigotry, fundamentalism and fanaticism, greed and jealousy, whether among individuals, groups, or nations are corrosive emotions that must be overcome as we move into the next century; and that love and compassion, caring and charity, friendship and cooperation are the elements that have to be encouraged as we transit into our new global awareness.

4. That the world's great religions must no longer war against each other for supremacy, but mutually cooperate for the welfare of the human race, and that through a continuing and creative interfaith dialogue the golden thread of spiritual aspiration that binds them together must be nurtured instead of feeding the dogma and exclusivism that divides them.

5. That a new, holistic education must acknowledge the multiple dimensions of the human personality—physical, intellectual, aesthetic, emotional, and spiritual—and seek a harmonious development of the integrated human being.

Ever since I first saw it two decades ago, I have been fascinated by the amazing photograph taken from the moon showing our planet as it really is—a tiny speck of light and life, so beautiful and yet so fragile, ablaze with the fire of consciousness against the blackness of outer space. This Earth, looked upon in so many cultures as the Mother, has nurtured the evolution of consciousness from the slime of the primeval ocean billions of years ago to where we stand today. Now, in a dramatic reversal, it is we who must nurture this Earth, to repair the scars that in our hubris we have inflicted upon her and safeguard the welfare of all creatures that inhabit her today and in millennia to come. This further evolution of our consciousness must surely be the guiding vision for all of us in the attempt to structure a humane society in the early twenty-first century.

Thomas Berry . . . on the historical mission of our times

I summarize my own thinking in a single sentence with seven phrases: The historical mission of our times is to reinvent the human at the species level, with critical reflection, within the community of life systems, in a time-developmental context, by means of story and shared dream experience.

First, I say "reinvent the human" because the issues we are concerned with seem beyond the competence of our present cultural traditions. As human more than any other mode of being, we give shape and form to ourselves in our cultural configurations. We are genetically coded toward a further transgenetic coding whereby we articulate the human mode of being. We are genetically coded to think. We do not have a choice to think or not to think. We do have a choice of *what* we think and *how* we shape our patterns of living, our moral codes, our social institutions, and our artistic and literary traditions. What is needed is something beyond our existing traditions to bring us back to the most fundamental aspect of the human. The issue has never been as critical as it is now. The human is at an impasse. We have been using our freedom of determination to set ourselves at odds with the entire nonhuman community of earthly existence. We need to give a cultural form to ourselves that is coherent with the larger community of existence.

Second, we must work "at the species level" because our problems are beyond any existing cultural solution. We must return to our genetic coding. Our problems are at the species and interspecies level. This is clear in every aspect of the human. As regards economics, we need not simply a national or a global economy but a species and interspecies economy. Presently our schools of business teach the skills whereby the greatest possible amount of natural resources is processed as quickly as possible, put through the consumer economy, and then passed on to the junk heap where it is useless at best and toxic to every living being at worst. There is need for the human species to develop reciprocal economic relationships with other life forms providing a sustaining pattern of mutual support, as is the case with other life systems.

As regards law, we need a species legal tradition that would provide for the legal rights of geological and biological as well as human components of the Earth community. A legal system exclusively for humans is not realistic. Habitat, for example, must be given legal status as sacred and inviolable for every mode of being.

Third, "with critical reflection" because this reinventing of the human needs to be done with critical competence. We need all our scientific knowledge. We cannot abandon our technologies. We must, however, see that our technologies cohere to the technologies of the natural world. Our knowledge needs to be a creative response to the natural world rather than a domination of the natural world.

Fourth, we need to reinvent the human "within the community of life systems." Because the Earth is not adequately understood either by our spiritual or by our scientific traditions, the human has become an addendum or an intrusion. We have found this situation to our liking because it enables us to avoid the problem of integral presence to the Earth. This attitude prevents us from considering the Earth as a single society with ethical relations determined primarily by the well-being of the total Earth community.

But while the Earth is a single integral community, it is not a global sameness. It is highly differentiated in bioregional communities—in arctic as well as tropical regions, in mountains, valleys, plains, and coastal regions. These bioregions can be described as identifiable geographical areas of interacting life systems that are relatively self-sustaining in the ever-renewing processes of nature. As the functional units of the planet, these bioregions can be described as self-propagating, self-nourishing, self-educating, self-governing, self-healing and self-fulfilling communities.

Fifth, reinventing the human must take place in "a time-developmental context." We now understand the universe and the planet Earth not simply as an ever-renewing sequence of seasonal transformations; it is also an emergent process going through an irreversible sequence of transformation episodes, moving in general from lesser to greater complexity in structure, from lesser to greater modes of consciousness, from lesser to greater freedoms. This constitutes what might be called the cosmological dimension of the program of the Club of Budapest. Our sense of who we are and what our role is must begin where the universe begins. Not only our physical shaping but also our spiritual and cultural shaping begins with the formation of the universe.

Sixth, from the above we can appreciate the directing and energizing role played by "the story of the universe." This story that we know through empirical observation is our most valuable resource in establishing a viable mode of being for the human species as well as for all those stupendous life systems whereby the Earth achieves its grandeur, its fertility, and its capacity for continuing self-renewal. This story—as told in its galactic expansion, its Earth formation, its life emergence, and its consciousness manifestation in the human—fulfills in our times the role of the mythic accounts of the universe that existed in earlier times when human awareness was dominated by a spatial mode of consciousness. We have moved from cosmos to cosmogenesis, from the mandala journey to the center of an abiding world, to the great irreversible journey of the universe itself as the primary sacred journey.

This journey of the universe is the journey of each individual being in the universe. The great journey is an exciting revelatory story that gives us our macrophase identity—the larger dimensions of meaning that we need. To be able to identify the microphase of our being with the macrophase mode of our being is the quintessence of what needs to be achieved.

The present imperative of the human is that this journey continue on into the future in the integrity of the unfolding life systems of the Earth, which presently are threatened in their survival. Our great failure is the termination of the journey for so many of the most brilliant species of the life community. The horrendous fact is that we are, as Norman Myers has indicated, in an extinction spasm that is likely to produce "the greatest single setback of life's abundance and diversity since the first flickerings of life almost four billion years ago." The labor and care expended over some billion years and untold billions of experiments to bring forth such a gorgeous Earth may be negated within something more than a century mistakenly considered progress toward a better life in a better world.

The seventh and final aspect of my statement concerning the ethical imperative of our times is the "shared dream experience." The creative process, whether in the human or the cosmological order, is too mysterious for easy explanation. Yet we all have experience of creative activity. Human processes involve much trial and error, with only occasional success at any high level of distinction, and we may well believe that the cosmological process has also passed through a vast period of experimentation in order to achieve the ordered processes of our present universe.

In both instances something is perceived in a dim and uncertain manner, something radiant with meaning that draws us on to a further clarification of our understanding and our activity. Suddenly out of the formless condition a formed reality appears. This process can be described in many ways, as a groping or as a feeling or as an imaginative process. The most appropriate way of describing this process seems to be that of dream realization. The universe appears to be the fulfillment of something so highly imaginative and so overwhelming that it must have been dreamed into existence.

But if the dream is creative, we must also recognize that few things are so destructive as a dream or entrancement that has lost the integrity of its meaning and become an exaggerated and destructive manifestation. This has happened often enough with political ideologies and with religious visionaries, but there is no dream or entrancement in the history of the Earth that has wrought the destruction taking place in the entrancement with industrial civilization. Such entrancement must be considered as a profound cultural pathology. It can be dealt with only by a correspondingly deep cultural therapy. This healing therapy can be successful only if associated with a creative vision capable of giving birth to a new more integral expression of the entire planetary process.

Such is our present situation. We are involved not simply with an ethical issue but with a disturbance sanctioned by the very structures of the culture itself in its present phase. The destructive dream of the twentieth century appears as a kind of ultimate manifestation of that deep inner rage of Western society against its earthly condition as a vital member of the life community. As with the goose that laid the golden egg, so the Earth is assaulted in a vain effort to possess not simply the magnificent fruits of the Earth but the power itself whereby these splendors have emerged.

At such a moment a new revelatory experience is needed, an experience wherein human consciousness awakens to the grandeur and sacred quality of the Earth process. This awakening is our human participation in the dream of the Earth, the dream that is carried in its integrity not in any one of Earth's cultural expressions but in the depths of our genetic coding. Therein the Earth functions at a depth beyond our capacity for conscious awareness. We can only be sensitized to what is revealed to us. Such participation in the dream of the Earth we probably have not had since our earlier shamanic times, but therein lies our hope for the future for ourselves and the entire Earth community.

Robert Muller . . . on consciousness and the global emergency
In fifty years of world service with the United Nations, I have come to consider the birth of planetary consciousness, together with the

creation of global institutions and the convening of world conferences, the major hopes for enabling humanity to cope with the
acute problems facing us. In view of the current resistance, slow-
ness, if not opposition of many governments to act upon the various intergovernmental agreements on the environment, and being
a member of the Club of Budapest, I consider it my duty to make
the following recommendations:

1. To declare a state of emergency of the Earth;

2. To consider the present situation as an outright war: a World
   War III against nature and its elements, a war that must now end;

3. To request a second world conference on the biosphere, twenty
   years after the first one in 1978, to ascertain the state of the biosphere today;

4. To support the extension to other countries of the World Party
   of Natural Law already existing in eighty-five countries at the
   initiative of British scientists;

5. To place our weight behind a radical change in the political system of our planet, a system that provides services and financial
   resources ranging from local communities, cities, provinces, and
   nations but leaves the Earth and the human family almost
   entirely without adequate services and financial resources at a
   time when these are most urgently needed;

6. In view of the chaos of the nation-state system and its colossal
   duplication of services and their financial costs (e.g., the national
   military establishments), to urgently agree on the absolute and
   imperative necessity to create, whether sooner or later but
   unavoidably, a proper Earth Government either in the form of a
   Federal Government, of a United States of the World, of a Union
   based on the model of the European Union, of five continental
   Unions with a global superstructure, or of a Government pat-
   terned on bioregional or bio-organizational models suggested by
   nature herself.

In the absence of such initiatives, we are likely to see the disappearance of most life forms, including human life, from this planet in the course of the twenty-first century.

Riane Eisler . . . on partnership and the new consciousness

The human community faces an epochal challenge: how to bring about the changes in consciousness required if we are to have a more equitable and sustainable future. Human consciousness does not spring up in a vacuum: it is shaped by culture. That is why at this evolutionary crossroads—when we and our natural habitat are being, as never before, reshaped by technology—cultural evolution is as important as biological evolution, and in some ways more so.

Over the last three hundred years we have seen great changes in consciousness: challenges to beliefs and institutions that were not so long ago viewed as "just the way things are." These challenges were initiated by small, unpopular, and often persecuted minorities conscious that we humans have alternatives—that man's domination of nature, of women, and of "lesser" men is neither divinely ordained nor biologically prefigured.

As this consciousness spread, mass movements sprang up challenging the supposedly divinely ordained right of kings to rule their "subjects," of men to rule women and children in the "castles" of their homes, of "superior" races to rule "inferior" ones, of warlike tribes and nations to conquer more peaceful ones and, most recently, of our species to overpopulate, despoil, and pollute the planetary habitat.

Although we do not yet think of them in these terms, these movements are not random and disconnected, and neither is resistance to them. Underneath the currents and countercurrents of history lies the dynamic tension between two basic possibilities of human culture: partnership and domination. Each of these models has a very different configuration that is visible once we become conscious of a generally ignored interactive systems dynamic: that relations in the private and the public spheres are inextricably intertwined. In fact, it is through our intimate relations that we first learn, and then continually practice respect for, or violation of, human rights as well as respect for, or disregard of, the natural habitat. Through these relations that involve touch to the body, our intimate sexual relations as well as our early childhood relations, we internalize, on a deeply unconscious neurological level, how two bodies should relate. If we are to effectively change consciousness in the direction needed for human and planetary survival, it is necessary to address the critical matter of how consciousness is culturally formed and replicated.

One of the great challenges we face is how to awake contemporary consciousness to the possibility—and urgent necessity—of relations based primarily on partnership rather than domination, in both the private and the public sphere. In this regard we must dispel some prevailing myths about what is popularly called "human nature"—our biological constraints and possibilities. Despite myths that we humans are base, flawed by either original sin or selfish genes, the most profound human yearning rooted in our biological evolution is for caring connection. Indeed, despite our conditioning for thousands of years for dominator rather than partnership relations with one another and with nature, we have an inherent capacity, indeed an inherent drive, toward relations based on partnership. Despite beliefs and institutions that have rewarded, and even idealized cruelty and violence (as in our "heroic" epics), we have an enormous capacity for caring and for altruistic behaviors—as demonstrated, for example, by the women and men who during the Nazi era risked their lives and those of their families to save Jews. Notwithstanding myths that men naturally want to dominate women and women naturally want to be dominated, women and men worldwide have been moving toward relations based on partnership in both the public and the private sphere. Despite adages such as "spare the rod and spoil the child" and the notion that violence can be the instrument of our deliverance (still propagated by some fundamentalist religious authorities), the institution of war, as well as such institutionalized forms of intimate violence as wife and child beating, have been increasingly challenged. And, as this report shows, despite the continuing idealization of "man's conquest of nature," the consciousness of our interconnections with all forms of life on this planet is beginning to reemerge.

For the last three centuries we have seen a major revolution in consciousness: the emergence in bits and pieces of the consciousness that a partnership way of structuring human society and culture is a viable possibility. We have also begun to see the recognition of something else: that we humans are the only species we know of who have consciously attempted to create a more equitable and sustainable society—once again suggesting that not only is a partnership form of social organization essential at this point in our cultural and technological evolution but that it is the form we need if we are to develop our uniquely human potentials.

It is this emerging Holos consciousness—and the active efforts of each one of us to spread it through all our institutions, from the family and religion to politics, economics, education, and the mass media—that offers us realistic hope for our future and that of generations still to come.

Edgar Morin . . . on the evolutionary path

A globalized situation calls for a global response. Such a response will have to be prepared, initiated, and stimulated by local initiatives. We are in a dialectical movement of parts and wholes: the parts contribute to the whole. In this sense national states can play a decisive role—provided they accept, in their own interest, to abandon pretensions of absolute sovereignty with regard to the great issues of common interest, issues of life and death. These go far beyond their own national competence. The productive era of nation-states wielding absolute power is past. This does not mean that nation-states have to be disintegrated, rather, that they need to be integrated in greater wholes with regard to the vital imperatives of the planet of which they themselves are a part.

The issue is all the more crucial because, as an indirect consequence, the process of globalization gives rise to balkanization and national and ethnocentric recalcitrance. An evolutionary path can open up only in the dialectic of the local and the global, the national and the worldwide, out of the conjunction and synergy of various forces and tendencies progressing in a salutary direction. This path must allow:

1. The universal spread of the social providence of the state (which entails the de-bureaucratization of heavy state machinery).

2. The regulation or slowing of international economic competition. This presupposes the action of international, "trinitarian" (economic, ecologic, cultural) authorities equally competent to fight against ecological degradation as a result of uncontrolled growth as against cultural degradation due to sweeping westernization.

3. The design of a civilization-enhancing policy to halt the processes of destruction and self-destruction generated by the globalization of Western society. This policy needs to regenerate and foster the humanist, rational, civil, critical, and self-critical virtues that have also been created in this process, virtues that are necessary ingredients in the reform of civilization.

4. The emergence of a planetary citizenship with branches all over the world through humanitarian and ecologic associations and nongovernmental organizations concerned with development, the rights of women, the protection of minorities, and the like.

5. The strengthening of the consciousness of people that they belong to the Earth as our shared homeland. This Holos consciousness implies not only a keen awareness of our community and of our earthly destiny but also an awareness of our common origins and common identity. It constitutes unity in multiplicity in the biological and psychological as well as the cultural spheres. By rooting our consciousness in our belonging to the Earth-Homeland, we can develop a sense of responsibility and mutual solidarity, and civilize human relationships in all parts of the globe.

A new way of thinking is closely linked with a new consciousness. This does not mean that we have to "unalienate" ourselves
(to some extent we have to alienate ourselves from others to become
ourselves)—rather, it means that we have to disabuse ourselves of
egocentrism and ethnocentrism while safeguarding our roots.

Pir Vilayat Inayat Khan . . . on the awakening of consciousness

As humanity on Planet Earth becomes gradually (although all too
slowly) aware of its identity as a multiple whole, several nexuses are
forming in a vast network fashioned by minds scattered around the
globe—minds that are beginning to think globally because they are
concerned about the well-being of this magnificent planet, so seriously plundered by egoistic greed. The Club of Budapest figures
foremost among these. Evolution does not only entail an upsurge
of consciousness, as Pierre Teilhard de Chardin said, moving from
a narrow outlook to increasingly wider perspectives, but also the
awakening of consciousness from what one believes to be personal
interest to the interest of more and more beings, of the planet as a
whole, a magnificent being sacrificed by misconstrued personal
interest.

As the violation of our responsibility toward each other and
toward Gaia escalates to the danger point, forward-looking people
are sounding an alarm. That in many respects previous cries of
alarm have fallen on deaf ears because they would have curbed
vested interests arouses worry, foreboding, and outrage. We are
foreclosing the future of our grandchildren by jeopardizing their
inheritance, their share in what we have since abused.

We feel comforted that a growing number of men and women of
insight are trying to alert public opinion so that political powers
may gauge the political values at stake and muster the courage to
overcome the resistance of powerful economic and business groups.
But much damage is being done to the minds of the masses by the
kind of make-believe that consists of subverting genuine spiritual
experience by institutionalized religion so as to guarantee the

authoritarian status to religious leaders. This has led, and is still leading, to religious intolerance degenerating into political conflict, all in the name of religious tenets called "fundamentalist."

If at the pinnacle of the evolutionary advance of humanity a global vision and global identity are to form, then religious interchange must be regarded as one of the most critical issues—and now one of the major obstacles to this evolution. If indeed a global identity, identity as members of the human family, does not ignore the rich diversity of individuals, so a global religious understanding need not prove threatening to our faith in the rich variety of religious and cultural traditions. We must take the first step toward religious convergence, coordination, or communion in the sacred. I welcome dialogues with spiritual leaders to explore together the new perspectives for spirituality in this new millennium.

Ignazio Masulli . . . on species consciousness

We are called upon to take a step, historically unprecedented, one that cannot even be envisaged except through the attainment of a new phase of historical consciousness—a consciousness of ourselves as a species. Today, even life and the perpetuation of life have become problems of historical dimensions. The responsibility for evolution can no longer be left to the individual's instinctive defense mechanisms, which are presently the sole foundations of our value judgments. This responsibility has become a problem of historical decisions that involve the entire species.

Throughout much of its history, the evolution of the human species has gone hand in hand with attempts by society to defend itself against contingencies arising from natural calamities, as well as from threats originating in its internal environment. This has brought to the fore the forces of egotism, expressed in acts of domination and antagonism. The landscape of history is littered with unmistakable evidence of fiercely competitive behaviors in the form of weapons, fortifications, frontiers—all manner of instruments and symbols of power. Corresponding to these, in a nonmaterial guise, we find the no less rigid demarcations perpetrated by symbols of identity, sometimes superimposed on one another: the individual, the clan, the ethnic group, the nation, the race.

Today, these barriers and discriminations have become walls that imprison us. Given the current world problems with their global interdependences, all our will and energy will be required if we are to break down the walls we have been erecting around and within ourselves.

It is relevant here to recall Jonas Salk's warning: our future evolution will not be decided by the survival of the strongest but by the survival of the wisest. An essential anthropological drive, that of *Being*, must prevail over the pressures of the *Ego*. This is the transformation we are now called upon to undertake. Ervin Laszlo could hardly be clearer on this matter. I shall only emphasize three points here.

The first of these bears on the global nature of the problems facing us. Recent years have witnessed a large number of studies and debates, from institutional as well as other sources, regarding the critical disequilibrium caused by our exploitation and waste of natural resources, the demographic explosion, impacting above all on the poorest areas of the world, and the growing and ever more serious divide between wealth and poverty. And who among us has not experienced a sense of frustration, even outright pessimism, feeling that all the words expended on these subjects are scarcely likely to be followed by concrete action? What emerges from the pages of the report is its global vision. Nor is this merely a matter of placing one problem beside another. Rather, that vision derives from the ability to trace the problems back to their historical origins—that is, to the thought and action by which they were generated. From such a standpoint it is possible to envisage feasible solutions.

The second element, intimately connected with the first, is that Laszlo identifies the key points on which to act in order to achieve a new perspective. He speaks very clearly: the responses to the problems cannot be delegated to the traditional élites, whether economic, political, scientific, or other. They can only spring from a new consciousness, increasingly deep and embracing, which is to become the common property of the world's peoples. He states explicitly that although numerous innovative views for tackling problems of this kind have been produced by individuals and groups—though these are in a minority in the science community—they remain too far removed from public opinion. The new approaches are not made intelligible to the public, and the widely diffused conceptions have tended to become obsolete.

I might add that the diffusion of innovative views and approaches impacting on the consciousness of the majority entails a change in the relationship between science and society. No less significant is the warning to the economic and political élites that unless we rethink the ethics of economics and politics it will be impossible to obtain a different relationship between the power-holders and those affected by them. Room must be found for decisions that are not dictated by vested and regional interests. Inasmuch as we are required to make choices different from those that have gone before, our decisions must be directed toward the general objectives of humankind as a whole. This will only be possible if we recognize the truly fundamental requirements.

A third point concerns the quest for the sources of the new Holos consciousness. In this regard art and science are linked anew. Art is implicated because it is capable of plumbing the depth of the significance of the human condition and of the relationships that bind people with one another and to the living world as a whole. Science is implicated because it contributes toward recovering a unitary meaning of the world. These potentials of art and science need focused attention and careful development. The scientific revolution of the seventeenth century prepared the way for the amazing scientific and technical advances of our time, but it adopted instrumental and regional ways of thinking. It is the historical task of contemporary scientists to rebuild a unitary, organic conception of reality.

Otto Herbert Hajek . . . on the role of art and artists

Human society can only prevent the threatening self-destruction of itself and its world—through overpopulation, irresponsible exploitation of nature's raw materials, waste of energy, and damage to the biosphere—if it is prepared to evolve a new global ethics. This report states this insight clearly and convincingly. It is thus an intrinsic responsibility of art and artists to spread this insight so that it becomes the basis of the life of society and a reality for each individual human being.

Artistic engagement and self-assertion have to be measured by the effect that artistic products—whether individual works or social creations—trigger in the consciousness of the observer as well as of the public. Art creates a sense of solidarity. It awakens ideals and rearticulates our sense for humanely living together. It provides indications for all people to find their place in reality and to feel at home in it. Art deals with ideal models of the individual—models that in their aesthetic articulation become socially relevant. In doing so, it shows pathways for the future without moving beyond its own time. It creates active change in social value concepts and, through its questioning, sharpens our insights into social interconnections. Art creates meaning we can define as culture.

Art is able to meet the needs of people through aesthetic designs for humanely living together and dealing with the whole human being with respect to the ecology of the Earth. Through its images it frees our experience from an uncertain dullness, elevating it into consciousness. In our perception-deadening leisure culture, the claim of the individual to a world created by aesthetic imagination is manipulated and redirected to mere animation. My responsibility as an artist is to protect the image of the human being from himself.

Materialistic, cynical, antihuman decisions regarding scientific, technical, and political objectives become more insidious when supported by religious and cultural concepts. Twentieth-century German history, among others, has proven this to disastrous effect. The bloody conflicts and ethical purges in Yugoslavia also justify the reality of wars of cultures. An intolerant fundamentalism mobilizes exclusivist antiforeigner feelings and provides simplistic identifications for people lost in the globalized economic, political, and media structures of today's world.

I believe in the impact of art on social relations and on the valuation of our interconnections with and within our life systems. My own artistic and artistic-political activities have always focused on protecting and enhancing the basic rights of human beings—their cultural dimension. This dimension has to prevail against immature political decision-making and social constraints. Assessments in terms of GDP give no direction whatsoever—in today's vacuum "anything goes." Artists need a constructive way of thinking to help society put forward questions and no longer accept failure to receive answers.

Peter Roche . . . on what business "could" do

Alfred P. Sloan, a former Chairman and CEO of General Motors, is frequently quoted as having said, "The business of business is business." Not only has this statement been much quoted over time, it has been amplified and refined by successive business leaders, politicians, and scholars to the point where the role and jurisdiction of business has become clearly bounded—it is "business."

The accepted interpretation of the role of business, especially publicly owned businesses, has become to produce the maximum financial returns for stockholders. The job of business leaders in this context is creating the strategy, structure, products and services, and loyal customer base to reap "maximum financial returns."

Given that most leaders—board members and officers—of large publicly owned companies are also substantial stockholders, it is not too great a leap to suggest that what really motivates the leaders of business is personal self-interest. At some point in their careers the locus of that self-interest moves from just making the largest amount of money possible to creating a reputation for making the largest amount of money—which in turn makes more money.

Most businesses have vision, mission, and values statements, and many businesses actually intend them to shape their actions and behavior. Yet what is missing from these statements is a footnote reading, "The foregoing is in the service of our primary mission and value, which is to make as much money as possible so as to make ourselves as rich as possible—which is, after all, the most primary concern of business."

We need to wake up to the fact that our business model, and the activity it generates, is subordinating other societal concerns to money. We are lulled into the illusion that if we just grow and make more money everything will work out. We are either unconscious of the state we are in or naive enough to believe that making and spending ever more money in a free market capitalist economy is the ultimate panacea.

For business, one possibility is to simply endorse the current free market capitalist economy as the best we have and are likely to have and learn to live and deal with its present and future unwanted by-products. This means accepting that a few people get very rich—and over time get richer still—while the rest of the people get poorer.

Another possibility for business is to recognize that the system we now have is an artifact and, as such, accessible to alteration. Given that we could remake the current system, what possibilities are there for doing so? What is it that business could be doing, if it so wished? In light of this report's checklist of responsible management, I am suggesting that business could:

■ Reinvent its own fundamental context, its operating tenets, and its values and ethics. It could use as context for the reinvention that enterprises operate as an integral part of a complex adaptive system that also includes social systems, political systems, and ecological systems.

■ Make enterprises function as the primary means of ensuring that every person on the planet has sufficient resources to meet his or her needs for survival and health.

- Reinterpret what health and viability means for enterprises, governments, and nongovernmental organizations and articulate the conditions for health and viability so that only choices that satisfy them would be considered sound.

- Shift the work of enterprises engaged in leading-edge research and resource consumption from military and warfare undertakings to undertakings that preserve and enhance life.

- Have executives give, as a requirement of their office, a declaration of their commitments, codes of ethics, and values to their investors and stakeholders—a statement that articulates the socially contributing purpose of the enterprise so that the making of money becomes a means to an end rather than an end in itself.

- By agreement, put a limit on individual ownership. Although it could still be perfectly acceptable for individual business leaders to create as much wealth as they can, or want, after a certain level of personal ownership the surplus would have to be given away. This, rather than merely the amount of money accumulated, would be the standard for success in society.

- Value, acknowledge, and encourage social and volunteer work by considering it in the context of career advancement. Part of the training and development of people could concern their involvement in the democratic process, social responsibility, and environmental conservation.

- Distinguish between work as an economic necessity in which there is one measure of wealth (work that is necessary to provide for the needs of individuals and families) and work as a creative expression. The latter would have a different measure of wealth, computed in terms of its contribution to joy, spirit, relationship, and self-expression. Such work would build the individual's sense of self, family ties, community relationships, sense of nation, and connection with the rest of humankind.

■ Abandon classical management theories as inadequate for dealing with today's world. It could acknowledge that our attempt at "controlling" and "organizing" ourselves out of successive problems has not, and as most evidence suggests will not, work.

■ Make enterprises, even global players, democracies. The governance of each enterprise should include large areas where a majority vote is needed for certain actions to be taken. Widen the scope and number of topics on which stockowners need to vote before management can act. Authority, resources, and accountability could be delegated to local units chartered to serve their local constituency.

■ Make the global enterprise into a federation of small entities acting locally inside a global charter, operating in partnership with civic, governmental and nongovernmental organizations for the benefit of the whole community.

■ Widen the stock ownership of enterprises to include employees and other community stakeholders. Just as senior executives now earn stock options for performance, so could all stakeholders share in the wealth created by enterprises.

■ Invent a declaration of stakeholders rights and responsibilities as the context for conducting working relationships.

■ Invent a forum in which "unworkability" is resolved in the framework of a commitment that the whole system should work. It could relate to "unworkability" as a threat to the viability of "space-station Earth," a threat against which everyone has a role to play and an interest in resolving.

This list of things to do is far from exhaustive. However, no amount of "could do's" will make a difference in reality without a fundamental reexamination of the context and role of business in society: its operating tenets, values, ethics, and the outcomes it produces. The call is to business leaders, politicians, scholars, and all who have a stake in the workability of enterprises to join in an "inquiry in action," designed to expand the benefits of business and to eliminate its damaging impacts.

Gary Zukav . . . on the unprecedented evolutionary transformation

The human species has entered a period of profound, fundamental, and unprecedented change. Its perceptual capability is expanding beyond the five senses. It is acquiring the ability to see itself as part of a larger fabric of life. The universe is becoming visible to it as a spiritual enterprise rather than a material one.

Until recently, humankind has been limited in its perception to the five senses and has evolved through the exploration of the physical world. The new, emerging humanity is not limited to the perception of the five senses. It is highly intuitive, and its means of evolution is entirely different. The emerging humanity evolves through responsible choice. A responsible choice is a choice that produces consequences for which the chooser is willing to assume responsibility.

This changes everything. First, the perception of power is changing from the ability to manipulate and control to the alignment of the personality with the soul. Multisensory humans see themselves as more than minds and bodies. They see themselves as immortal souls evolving voluntarily in a special learning environment—the domain of the five senses. The perception of power as the ability to manipulate and control is neither appealing nor accurate to them. They see alignment of the personality with the soul as authentic power and responsible choice as the means of creating it. The evolutionary modality of the emerging humankind is the alignment of the personality with the soul through responsible choice.

Social activism apart from the creation of authentic power is the pursuit of external power—the attempt to impose one will upon another. The pursuit of external power produces only violence and destruction. What once served the evolution of humankind is now counterproductive and dangerous. Old ways of responding to the challenges of a life on Earth no longer work. The challenges have never been greater or more numerous: deteriorating control of nuclear weapons, massive pollution, rapid extinction of species and cultures, increasing violence, a longer human life span, and an exponentially increasing human population with a finite resource base to support it.

The old ways are manipulation and control with the assistance of the intellect. The new ways—and the only ones that now offer humankind a future—are responsible choices of harmony, cooperation, sharing, and reverence for life with the assistance of the heart.

Any cause that identifies a villain contributes to the problem, not to its solution. The problem is internal—only its ramifications are external. The external mirrors the internal. No effort to change the reflection will change the source of the reflection. No war to end wars will end war, nor ever has. No campaign against greed will end avarice unless it is waged where the greed lives—in the heart of the campaigner. Every change requires a change in consciousness. This has always been the case. Now humankind is developing the ability to recognize and cooperate with this dynamic.

This is the unprecedented evolutionary transformation that is under way: the expansion of human consideration beyond its own needs into the limitless universe of wisdom and compassion of which it is part. It is our emerging ability to collaborate, for the first time as a species, with nonphysical yet real forms of life that are in advance of our own. It is partnering with the universe in the most conscious and responsible ways and the joy and fulfillment that result. It is radical personal responsibility for the whole through self-cultivation of compassion and kindness—through the pursuit of authentic power. At the heart of this endeavor is cultivation of the consciousness that is required. This is for each individual to undertake and complete. It is the greatest challenge and joy that now fills our lives.

Postscript

The Holistic Paradigm in Science

C UTTING-EDGE SCIENCE merits acquaintance by the widest lay-ers of the public. This is not only because science in its latest development conveys the best insight we possess to date about the nature of life and universe but also because the insight it conveys is of great practical relevance: it supports and legitimizes the basic features of Holos consciousness.

The new conceptions coming to the fore in physics, biology, cosmology, and consciousness research leave behind the mechanistic and fragmented view of the world. The leading researchers have uncovered tangible evidence for the kind of wholeness and interconnection that young people, and sensitive persons of all ages, perceive intuitively in their life and experience.

The Emerging Holism of Physics*

Classical physics was mechanistic and atomistic. It reposed on Newton's uncontested laws of nature, published in his *Philosophiae Naturalis Principia Mathematica* in 1687. These laws and the system in which they are stated became the foundation of modern-age Logos, the mechanistic worldview that achieved its fullest expression in the

---

* The scientific materials included here are based on Ervin Laszlo, *The Creative Cosmos* (Floris Books, Edinburgh, 1993), *The Interconnected Universe* (World Scientific, Singapore and London, 1994), *The Whispering Pond* (Element Books, Shaftesbury and Boston, 1997-98), and the most recent *Wholeness in Cosmos and Consciousness* (in press).

industrial civilization of the twentieth century. They demonstrated with geometrical certainty that material bodies are made up of mass points and that they move according to mathematically expressible rules on Earth, while planets rotate in accordance with Kepler's laws in the heavens. They showed that the motion of all masses is fully determined by the conditions under which motion is initiated, just as the motion of a pendulum is determined by its length and its initial displacement and the motion of a projectile is determined by its launch angle and acceleration.

Classical physics is not the physics of our day, however. Although Newtonian laws apply to objects moving at modest speeds on the surface of the Earth, the conceptual framework by which these motions, as all observed phenomena, are embedded has shifted radically. Today the fundamental units of the physical world are said to be intrinsically and instantly "entangled" with each other, creating subtle strands of connection that span the cosmos.

The classical conception of nature had begun to crumble by the end of the nineteenth century. The supposedly indivisible atom proved fissionable to a bewildering variety of components that, decades later, dissolved in a swirl of energy. Max Planck discovered that light, like all energy, comes not in a continuous stream but in discrete packets called quanta. Faraday and Maxwell came up with theories of nonmaterial phenomena such as electromagnetic fields, and Einstein advanced the special and the general theories of relativity.

The death-knell of the classical concepts was sounded in the 1920s with the advent of quantum mechanics, the physics of the ultra-small domains of reality. The quanta of light and energy that surfaced in ever more sophisticated experiments refused to behave like commonsense macroscale objects. Their behavior proved to be more and more weird. Einstein, who received the Nobel prize for his work on the photoelectric effect (where streams of light quanta are generated on irradiated plates), did not suspect, and was never ready to accept, the weirdness of the quantum world. But physicists investigating the behavior of these packets of light and energy found that, until registered by an instrument of detection or another act of observation, quanta have no specific position, nor do they occupy a unique state. It appears that the ultimate units of physical reality have no uniquely determinable location, and they exist in a superposition of several potential states at the same time.

Compared with the realistic tenets of Newtonian physics, the world of the quantum appears weird indeed. Unlike Newton's mass points, unambiguously definable in terms of force, position, and motion, the definition of the state of the quantum has to be given by a wave function that encodes the superposition of all the states the quantum can potentially occupy. A quantum of light or energy (and subsequently, also of force) is indeterminate as to the choice between these states. Moreover, it manifests properties either as a wave or as a particle, but not as both. Its properties cannot be measured all at the same time: for example, if one measures position, energy becomes blurred; and if one measures energy, position becomes indistinct. As soon as it is observed, the quantum's indeterminate state becomes determinate: it "chooses" one of its potential states. Physicists say that its superposed wave function collapses into the determinate state of the classical particle.

What the weirdness of the quantum means in terms of our knowledge of the universe has been debated for more than seventy years. The main points were made by pioneering theoreticians such as Nils Bohr, Werner Heisenberg, Louis de Broglie, and Erwin Schrödinger. Bohr advanced the principle of complementarity: a quantum has two complementary aspects, wave and particle, and whether it appears as a wave or as a particle depends on the kinds of questions we ask and the kinds of observations we make. Heisenberg put forward the "principle of uncertainty" which tells us that at any given time only one aspect of the quantum is measurable; a complete description is forbidden by nature. But the physical reasons for complementarity and for the interdiction of full determination remained a mystery. According to Bohr, the very question whether "in itself" the quantum is a wave or a particle is not a meaningful question and should not be asked. Quantum physics seemed compelled to deal, in Eugene Wigner's telling phrase, with *obser-vations* rather than with *observables*.

Einstein was far from happy with this state of affairs and suggested that something is missing in the observational and theoretical arsenal of quantum physics; in some essential respects it is incomplete. Einstein's one-time student and collaborator David Bohm sought to fill the gap by introducing "hidden variables"—classical causal factors that would operate in nature hidden from observation and account for the weirdness of the quantum state. Others sought explanations that link the observations to the observer. They pointed out that any observation requires at the minimum that some light is bounced off the object examined, and in the case of an "object" as minuscule as a quantum this means interfering with it—giving it a "momentum kick." This collapses the wave function: the multiple-potentiality wave aspect of the quantum vanishes and yields to the classical particle aspect. It is for this reason that the observed world around us is "classical"—the wave functions in it are constantly collapsed.

Until the 1980s, quantum weirdness had to be accepted, and the best physicists could do was to point to the smooth functioning of the equations by which quantum theorists compute the observations and make predictions. Explanations as to what the phenomena themselves were were forbidden to physicists (by the Copenhagen school of quantum physics founded by Bohr), as they were considered "philosophical"—excessively speculative. But in the last two decades of the twentieth century the picture began to change.

Understanding the latest insights requires that we go back to the experiments pioneered by Thomas Young in the beginning of the nineteenth century. Young made coherent light pass through an intervening surface with two slits. (He created coherent light by allowing sunlight to pass through a pinhole; today, lasers are used for this purpose.) A screen is placed behind the intervening surface to receive the light that penetrates through the slits. As experiment after experiment testifies, a wave-interference pattern appears on the screen. The same effect can be observed on the bottom of a pool when two drops or pebbles are made to disturb the sunny and otherwise smooth surface of the water. The waves spreading from each disturbance meet and interfere with each other: where the crest of one wave meets the crest of the other, they reinforce each other and appear bright. Where crest meets trough, they cancel each other and appear dark. The common-sense explanation is that light quanta have the property of waves: they pass through both slits. This, however, becomes problematic when the light source is so weak that only one photon is emitted at a time: as a corpuscular particle the photon could only pass through one of the slits. Nevertheless, when seemingly corpuscular photons are emitted one after another, a wave-interference pattern is built up on the screen.

Photons passing through one slit interfere with each other as if they passed through both. Is the photon a particle when emitted, and a wave when passing through the slits? Does it interfere with itself? On the other hand, as soon as a determination is made as to which of the two slits the photon (or electron or atom) is passing through, the interference pattern disappears. The wave function collapses.

Recent experiments shed fresh light on the nature of this puzzling phenomenon. It appears that only a coherent light beam produces the interference pattern—ordinary light behaves as a stream of Newtonian particles, illuminating the screen as a diffuse brightness. But coherence is extremely fragile: any interference with the light beam destroys it. As soon as any part of the experimental apparatus is coupled with the source of the photons, their superposed quantum state vanishes, yielding the classical state. In experiments designed to determine through which of the slits a given photon passes, the "which-path detector" gives the photon a "momentum kick." This collapses the wave function, whether or not anyone observes it. A physical process appears to be at work here: the coupling of the measuring apparatus to the light source.

But the quantum is weirder than that: it turns out that the wave function collapses (for the interference pattern disappears) even in the absence of an actual interaction between the which-path detector and the light source. In one experiment (Leonard Mandel's optical-interference experiment of 1991) a sophisticated pretuning of the quanta ensures that its path through one or the other of the slits can be detected. Astonishingly, the interference pattern disappears even when the detector is not turned on. It seems that the very possibility of "which-path-detection" destroys the superposed-state associated with the otherwise intact photons. This was confirmed in the fall of 1998, when University of Konstanz physicists Dürr, Nunn, and Rempe reported that the wave function collapses also when detection is made by instrumentation so fine that its effect is too small to account for the vanishing of the interference pattern (the "back action" path of the detector is four orders of magnitude smaller than the separation of the wave fringes). The apparatus does not deliver the "momentum kick" previously required to convert the quantum to the classical state, yet the conversion occurs just the same.

These experiments, which can be performed whether or not anyone is watching, do away with the notion that a conscious observer would collapse the wave function (a hypothesis advanced among others by Eugene Wigner). And they also do away with interaction as the necessary condition of the collapse—it occurs in its absence as well. But if so, to what would it be due?

One answer is that a faster-than-light signal is passing between the which-path detector and the photons (or electrons or atoms) that traverse the slits. However, such signaling violates the relativistic limitation on the speed of light, and it does not carry information in any meaningful sense of the term. There is another explanation, however, which at first glance is just as mysterious as a supraluminal signal, but is more consistent with the facts. It is that *the states of the detector apparatus and of the light source are instantly and intrinsically correlated.*

The idea of instant and intrinsic correlation goes back to a concept advanced by Erwin Schrödinger in the 1930s. It is "entanglement." Entanglement does away with the weirdness of the photon emitted by a light source seemingly "knowing" that its path is detected (or merely that it is detectable). Physicists and physical cosmologists are coming to the realization that the states of all quanta in the universe are intrinsically entangled with each other. This suggests that in its totality the physical universe is an intrinsically and instantaneously interconnected whole—a far cry from the Newtonian universe of mechanically interacting independent mass points.

The Emerging Holism of Biology

For the better part of the past two centuries holism in biology was considered idealistic or metaphysical. It was associated with vitalism (the concept that life is infused with a vital force or energy), or teleology (the notion that life and evolution tend toward a predetermined goal or "telos"). Reacting to these nineteenth-century ideas, twentieth-century biologists turned to the contrary approach, which was to emulate classical physics in viewing the organism as a complex mechanism. Investigators claimed that the organism can be understood as a collection of independent if interacting parts, such as cells, organs, or organ systems. These can be analyzed individually, and the analysis can show how their interaction produces the functions and manifestations of life in the organism. The analytic approach gave rise to molecular biology and modern genetics and encouraged the current trend toward genetic engineering. The initial success of these methods and technologies seemed to have provided sufficient proof of the correctness of the approach from which they sprang.

However, in the late twentieth century the mechanistic conception of life came to be increasingly questioned. Innovative biologists noted that the alternative to mechanism is not a return to vitalism and teleology but adopting an organismic approach. This has been explored as a philosophy by the great process thinkers of the late nineteenth and early twentieth century, such as Henri Bergson,

Samuel Alexander, Lloyd Morgan, and Alfred North Whitehead. The latter's concept of the organism as a fundamental metaphor for all entities of the physical and the living world served as the rallying point for the post-Darwinian developmental schools of the new biology.

The developmental approach maintains that organisms have a level and form of integrity that cannot be fully understood merely by studying their parts and their interaction. The concept "the whole is more than the sum of its parts" holds, for when the parts are integrated within the living organism, properties emerge and processes take place that are not the simple sum of the properties or aggregate of the processes of the parts. The living organism cannot be reduced to the interaction of its parts without losing its "emergent properties"—the very characteristics that make it living.

"Coherence" is the concept that best expresses the wholeness now discovered in the domains of life. Coherence is not an exclusively biological notion: it exists in the mechanistic context as well. For example, a well functioning mechanism, such as a finely engineered car or airplane, can be said to be coherent. But the organically coherent system, unlike a mechanically coherent one, is not decomposable to its component parts and levels of organization. In the words of biophysicist Mae Wan Ho, the organically coherent system is dynamic and fluid, its myriad activities self-motivated, self-organizing, and spontaneous, engaging all levels simultaneously from the microscopic and molecular all the way to the macroscopic. There are no controlling parts or levels, and no parts or levels controlled. The applicable concept is not *control* but *communication*. Thanks to the constant communication of the parts in the organism, adjustments, responses, and changes required for the maintenance of the whole can propagate in all directions at once.

For the understanding of the nature of organic coherence, Ho suggests that a great dance group or a good jazz band is a useful example. Here all performers are perfectly in tune with each other and with the performance, and even the audience becomes one with the dance and the music. The "song and dance" within the living organism ranges over more than seventy octaves, with localized chemical bonds vibrating, molecular wheels turning, microcilia beating, fluxes of electrons and protons propagating, and metabolites and ionic currents within and among cells flowing through ten orders of spatial magnitude.

Similarly to the entanglement of quanta in the physical world, in organic coherence there are intrinsic and instant correlations, enabling changes to propagate throughout the living organism, making even distant sites neighboring. This is incompatible with the mechanistic concept of the organism, where the parts are separate from one another, having definite boundaries and simple location in homogeneous space and time.

Coherence in the living realm ranges from the smallest element in an organism to the full range of life on the planet. It encompasses multi-enzyme complexes inside cells, the organization of cells into tissues and organs, the polymorphism of living species within ecological communities, and the web of local and continental ecologies in the biosphere. It ensures the coordination of the biosphere's myriad organic and ecological systems and their coevolution.

The new concept of the evolution of life is considerably different from the classical concept. The latter maintains that biological evolution results from the interplay of two mutually independent factors: the genetic information encoded within the organism (the genome) and the physical organism in which that information is expressed (the phenome). The genome mutates randomly, and the phenome it codes is exposed to a succession of independently evolving environments. There, natural selection weeds out the unfit species and allows the fit to survive and reproduce.

The embracing concept of coherence in the living realm contradicts the mechanistic assumption of chance processes occurring among independent elements. The new concept is more than a philosophical or metaphysical tenet: there is increasing evidence that pure chance, which requires the complete absence of causal links, is not a significant factor in the evolution of life.

The evidence against the role of chance processes in evolution is wide-ranging. Random mutations are unable to explain even the earliest phases of biological evolution—complex structures have appeared within astonishingly brief periods of time. The oldest rocks date from about 4 billion years, and the earliest and already highly complex forms of life (blue-green algae and bacteria) are more than 3.5 billion years old. The classical theory cannot explain how this level of complexity could have emerged within the relatively short period of about 500 million years: a random mixing of the molecular soup would have taken incomparably longer to produce it.

The mechanistic chance-based process of mutation and natural selection likewise cannot account for the increasingly complex multicellular organisms that emerged in the course of time. The assembly even of a primitive self-replicating prokaryote (primitive non-nucleated cell) involves building a double helix of DNA consisting of some 100,000 nucleotides, with each nucleotide containing an exact arrangement of thirty to fifty atoms, together with a bi-layered skin and the proteins that enable the cell to take in food. This construction requires an entire series of reactions finely coordinated with each other.

Random mutations and natural selection may account for variations within a given species, but the roughly four billion years available on this planet for the evolution of biological complexity could not have been sufficient for these processes to generate today's complex and ordered organisms from their protozoic ancestors. This is because it is not enough for genetic mutations to produce one or a few positive changes in a species; they must produce the full set. The evolution of feathers, for example, does not make for a reptile that can fly; radical changes in musculature and bone structure are also required, along with a faster metabolism to power sustained flight. Each innovation by itself is not likely to offer evolutionary advantage; on the contrary, it is likely to make an organism less fit than the standard form from which it departed. And if so, it would soon be eliminated by natural selection. As a result, a random step-wise elaboration of the genetic code of a species is astronomically unlikely to produce viable results. Mathematical physicist Fred Hoyle pointed out that evolution occurring purely by chance is about as likely as a hurricane blowing through a scrap yard assembling a working airplane.

Life, it appears, comes about by massive and highly coordinated innovations in the genome, rather than by piecemeal variations dictated by chance. If there is no hidden program guiding evolution—a now abandoned teleological thesis—then in some way the environment in which the organism finds itself must be creating a "selection pressure" that limits and orients the genome's mutations.

There is growing evidence for this hypothesis. Experiments in Japan and the United States have shown that rats that developed diabetes when the insulin-producing cells of their pancreas were damaged by a drug administered in the laboratory had offspring in which diabetes arose spontaneously. It appears that the alteration of the rats' somatic cells produced corresponding alterations in the DNA of their germline. In some cases mutations are specifically correlated with the fields or chemicals that affect the organism. This is demonstrated by experiments with genetic mutations induced in bacteria. When particular genes of a strain of bacteria are rendered defective in the laboratory, some bacteria mutate back precisely those genes that the scientists made inoperative. And when some plants and insects are subjected to toxic substances, they mutate their genome in precisely such a way as to detoxify the toxins and create resistance to them. This is the phenomenon of pesticide resistance—a classic case of feedback regulation in the complex network (or "ecology") of genes that governs the organism. Because of this feedback, when bacteria or plants are exposed to sublethal levels of toxic substances, they need not wait for random mutations to occur. The genetic changes that come about are part and parcel of the physiological responses common to all cells challenged with toxic substances, including pesticides in plants, antibiotics in bacteria, and anticancer drugs in mammalian cells.

Scientists find that no gene works in isolation: the function of each gene is dependent on the context provided by all the others. The whole ecology of genes exhibits layers and layers of feedback regulation, originating both with the physiology of the organism and with its relationship to its environment. These regulations can change the function of the genes, rearrange them, make them move around, or even mutate them. Thus major mutations are not due to a haphazard recombination of genes but are flexible responses on the part of the genetic network of a living species to the chemical, climatic, and other changes successive generations of organisms experience in their milieu.

The emerging insight combines a long-discredited thesis of Jean Baptiste Lamarck (that the changes the organism experiences can be inherited) with a main pillar of the theory of Charles Darwin (that inheritance must always be mediated by the genetic structure of the organism). The influences an organism experiences in its milieu are indeed affecting subsequent generations—not because changes in the parent organism would be directly communicated to the offspring, but because some effects experienced by the parent organism leave their mark on its "ecology of genes" and are thus handed down from one generation to the next.

The discovery of subtle links between the genome and the organism, and between the whole organism and its environment, means that the living world is not the harsh domain of classical Darwinism, where each struggles against all, with every species, every organism, and every gene competing for advantage against every other. Rather, life evolves through what biologist Brian Goodwin calls the "sacred dance" of the living organism with its milieu. Subtle strains of that dance extend to all the species and ecologies in the biosphere.

In the emerging concept of the new biology, the web of life is just as intrinsically and thoroughly whole as the living organism—and as the world of the quantized particles that underlies them.

A FOOTNOTE TO THE
EVOLUTIONIST-CREATIONIST CONTROVERSY

Is the world the result of evolution or of design? The controversial (and subsequently revoked) decision of the Kansas State Board of Education to remove evolution from the state's science curriculum standards fanned the flames under this long-standing debate. The controversy heated up when each side accused the other of faulty reasoning and dubious morals. Yet a more constructive approach could be taken, because, notwithstanding appearances, the two positions—creationism on the one side and evolutionism on the other—are not mutually exclusive.

At first glance, the science community, and anyone believing that science discloses some basic truth about the nature of reality, is compelled to reject the creationist hypothesis. Things in this world are not the result of special acts of creation but of ongoing evolution. However, we must grant to the creationists that it is unlikely that everything we find around us, and indeed in us, is the result of chance processes. There must be more to this world than what the evolutionists claim.

This way of posing the issue is not just simple and straightforward but actually simplistic and considerably exaggerated. The view of evolution entertained by the creationists is the view held by mainline Darwinists, as articulated among others by Richard Dawkins—and at the leading edge this view is transcended. The living world, Dawkins claims, is the result of random processes based on trial and error, much like the work of a blind watchmaker. Contrary to appearances, there is no purpose in this world, and hence no need to assume purposeful design. For example, cheetahs give every indication of being superbly designed to kill antelopes. The teeth, claws, eyes, nose, leg muscles, backbone, and brain of a cheetah are all precisely what we should expect if God's purpose in creating cheetahs was to maximize deaths among antelopes. At the same time, antelopes are fast, agile, and watchful, apparently designed so they can escape cheetahs. Yet neither the one nor the other feature implies creation by special design: this is just the way nature is. Cheetahs have a "utility function" to kill antelopes, and antelopes, to escape cheetahs. Nature itself is indifferent to their fate. Ours is a world of blind physical forces and genetic replication, where some get hurt and others flourish. It has precisely the properties we would expect it to have if at bottom there was no design, no purpose, no evil and no good, only blind and pitiless indifference.

Evidently, if this were the case, it would be hard to believe in an intelligent Creator. The God that created it would have to be an indifferent God, if not actually a sadist who enjoys spectator blood sports. It is more reasonable, according to Dawkins, to hold that the world just is, without deeper reason or purpose. The way it is results from random processes played out within limits set by fundamental physical laws. The idea of design is superfluous. In this regard Darwinists echo French mathematician Pierre Laplace, who maintained that God is a hypothesis for which there is no longer any need.

Creationists, however, cannot accept that all we see in this world, ourselves included, should be the result of random processes and impersonal laws. The tenet that everything evolved by blind chance out of common and simple origins is mere theory, they say, unsubstantiated by solid evidence. Scientists cannot come up with manifest proof for this theory of evolution: "You can't go into the laboratory or the field and make the first fish," said Tom Willis, director of the Creation Science Association for Mid-America. The world around us is far more than a chance concatenation of disjoined elements; it exhibits meaning and purpose. This implies design.

The creationist position would make sense if the evolutionist position would be truly that of randomness and chance. It is not. In the new scientific view evolution is more than the outcome of chance mutations exposed to natural selection. The co-evolution of all things with all other things in the integral web of life is a systemic process with a built-in dynamic. It is part of the evolution of the universe from particles to galaxies and stars with planets. On this Earth this evolution produced physical, chemical, and thermal conditions that were just right for the stupendous processes of biological evolution to take off. Such conditions could only have come about in a universe governed by precisely coordinated laws and regularities. Even a minute change in these laws and constants would foreclose the emergence of life forever. The question cannot be avoided: how is it that this universe is so fortunately tuned that life can emerge in it? Is this the result of mere serendipity—or is it here that we finally encounter the traces of intelligent design?

The latter is more likely to be the case. The existence of stars and planets, microbes and organisms, does not call for special acts of creation: they can be accounted for by the self-evolution of the universe. But a universe capable of self-evolution does call for deeper explanation. The universe as a whole could not have come into existence due to natural causes; space and time themselves did not predate the universe but emerged when it was born. But if not natural causes, then what brought the universe and its laws into being?

The claim of serendipity faces a credibility gap. Physicist Roger Penrose calculated that some 10^{123} universes could have come into being other than our own—the laws and constants of our universe are that improbably fine-tuned to the evolution of life and complexity. If the universe was not specifically designed to permit the evolution of life and complexity, then reasoning based on statistical probability compels us to assume that there were 10^{123} tries before it was selected. There would then be a significant probability for its selection through trial or error.

The alternative to the "blind watchmaker" theory—not just of life but of the universe—is not the creationist thesis that everything in this world results from special acts of creation. If the universe is the way it is, science can explain how they have all come about through progressive evolution. But why is the universe the way it is? The real alternative to the random serendipity thesis is the the nonrandom creation of the laws and regularities that permit the universe to evolve itself.

A self evolving universe is far too remarkable to be the product of simple chance. Great scientists from Newton to Einstein have never contested this insight. Thus religion need not fight science, nor science laugh at religion. There is sufficient common ground for agreement—and for awe in the presence of a world that harbors the potentials to evolve itself from particles to planets, and microbes to minds.

The Emerging Holism of Consciousness Research

In their latest development the sciences of human mind and consciousness likewise paint a picture of subtle linkages and wholeness—a picture that encompasses human beings and the world around them.

In the conventional view we can perceive the external world only through our senses: everything that is in the mind is said to have been first in the eye. But psychologists, psychiatrists, and consciousness researchers are rediscovering what ancient cultures have always known: that we are capable of more subtle and spontaneous perceptions as well. Such spontaneous (and seemingly paranormal) phenomena are called "transpersonal." They furnish the evidence for holism in the sphere of mind and consciousness.

Experimental parapsychology laboratories produce impressive evidence of transpersonal forms of perception and interaction. Controlled tests on extrasensory perception (ESP) date from the 1930s, when J. B. Rhine conducted his pioneering card- and dice-guessing experiments at Duke University. Today's experimental designs are sophisticated and the experimental controls rigorous; physicists often join parapsychologists in carrying out the tests. A whole range of experimental protocols has been developed, from the noise-reduction technique known as the Ganzfeld technique to the highly respected DMILS (Distant Mental Influence on Living Systems) method. Explanations in terms of hidden sensory cues, machine bias, cheating by subjects, and experimenter incompetence or error have all been considered, but they were found unable to account for a number of statistically significant paranormal results. There appears to be an extremely subtle yet profound interconnection among living systems. In particular, human "senders" and "receivers" seem able to interact in ways that go beyond ordinary sense perception.

In the early 1970s two physicists, Russell Targ and Harold Puthoff, undertook a series of tests on thought and image transference. They placed the "receiver" in a sealed, opaque, and electrically shielded chamber, and the "sender" in another room where he or she was subjected to bright flashes of light at regular intervals. The brain-wave patterns of both sender and receiver were registered on electro-encephalograph (EEG) machines. As expected, the sender exhibited the rhythmic brain waves that normally accompany exposure to bright flashes of light. However, after a brief interval the receiver also began to produce the same patterns, although he or she was not being directly exposed to the flashes and was not receiving ordinary sense-perceivable signals from the sender.

Targ and Puthoff also conducted experiments on remote viewing. In these tests sender and receiver were separated by distances that precluded any form of sensory communication between them. At a site chosen at random, the sender acted as a "beacon," and the receiver tried to pick up what the sender saw. To document their impressions receivers gave verbal descriptions, sometimes accompanied by sketches. Independent judges found the descriptions and the sketches matched the characteristics of the site actually seen by the sender, on average, 66 percent of the time.

More recently two other physicists, Peter Stewart and Michael Brown in England, joined with Helen Stewart, a university administrator in New York, to test the reliability of a telepathic procedure "channeled" by Jane Roberts in her books on Seth. Transpersonal communication was attempted across the Atlantic in fourteen accurately timed sessions between April and September 1994. Detailed records of the observations and impressions were made via e-mail after each experiment, and they were stored on automatically dated and timed disks. Though the "clairvoyant" images were described in terms of associations rather than exact pictorial reproductions of the images seen by the sender, on the whole they corresponded to those images. The picture of a meteor shower, for example, came through as a snowstorm, the image of a tower with a rotating restaurant on top was picked up as a globe on a stand. Static images as well as dynamic sequences of images have been received—"still pictures" as well as "moving pictures."

Remote viewing experiments reported from other sources and laboratories involved various distances, ranging from half a mile to several thousand miles. Regardless of where they are carried out and by whom, the success rate was generally above random probability. The most successful viewers proved to be those who were relaxed, attentive, and meditative. They reported having received a preliminary impression as a gentle and fleeting form that gradually evolved into an integrated image. They experienced the image as a surprise, both because it was clear and because it was clearly elsewhere.

Another example of transpersonal communication came from the laboratory of Jacobo Grinberg-Zylberbaum at the National University of Mexico. In more than fifty experiments performed over five years, Grinberg-Zylberbaum paired his subjects inside sound- and electromagnetic radiation-proof "Faraday cages." He asked them to meditate together for twenty minutes, then he placed them in separate Faraday cages where one subject was stimulated and the other not. The stimulated subject received stimuli at random intervals in such a way that neither he or she nor the experimenter knew when they were applied. The subjects who were not stimulated remained relaxed, with eyes closed, instructed to feel the presence of the partner without knowing anything about his or her stimulation.

In general, a series of one hundred stimuli were applied, such as flashes of light, sounds, or short, intense, but not painful electric shocks to the index and ring fingers of the right hand. The electroencephalogic (EEG) brain-wave records of both subjects were then synchronized and examined for "normal" potentials evoked in the stimulated subject and "transferred" potentials in the nonstimulated person. Transferred potentials were not found in control situations without a stimulated subject, when a screen prevented the stimulated subject from perceiving the stimuli (such as light flashes), or when the paired subjects did not previously interact. But during experimental situations with stimulated subjects and with prior contact among them, the transferred potentials appeared consistently in about 25 percent of the cases. A particularly poignant example was furnished by a young couple, deeply in love; their EEG patterns remained closely synchronized throughout the experiment, testifying that their report of feeling deep oneness was not an illusion.

In a limited way, Grinberg-Zylberbaum could also replicate his results. When one individual exhibited the transferred potentials in one experiment, he or she usually exhibited them in subsequent experiments also. The results did not depend on spatial separation between senders and receivers—no matter how far or near they were to each other, the transfer effects remained the same.

An experiment I witnessed in person measured the degree of harmonization of the EEG waves emitted by the brains of different subjects. In ordinary waking consciousness the two hemispheres of the brain—the language-oriented, linearly thinking rational "left brain" and the Gestalt-perceiving intuitive "right brain"—exhibit uncoordinated, randomly diverging EEG patterns. When a person enters a meditative state, these patterns tend to become synchronized, and in deep meditation the two hemispheres often fall into a nearly identical pattern. The experiment in question—carried out by Italian physician and brain researcher Nitamo Montecucco—showed that in deep meditation not only the left and right brains of one and the same subject, but also the left and right brains of *different* subjects, manifest identical patterns. Tests with up to twelve meditating persons disclosed a close synchronization of the EEG waves of the entire group—even though there was no sensory contact among its members.

In addition to images and brain wave patterns, a variety of physiological effects also can be transmitted in the transpersonal mode. Transmissions of this kind came to be known as "telesomatic": they consist of physiological changes triggered in a targeted person by the mental processes of another. Some effects recall the quasi-mythical processes anthropologists call "sympathetic magic." Shamans, witch doctors, and other practitioners of sympathetic magic act not on the person they target but on an effigy of that person, such as a doll. This practice is widespread among traditional peoples; the rituals of Native Americans make use of it as well. In his famous study *The Golden Bough*, Sir James Frazer noted that Native American shamans would draw the figure of a person in sand, ashes, or clay and then prick it with a sharp stick or do it some other injury. The corresponding injury was believed to be inflicted on the person the figure represented. Observers found that the targeted person often fell ill, became lethargic, and would sometimes die. Dean Radin and his collaborators at the University of Nevada decided to test the positive variant of this effect under controlled laboratory conditions.

In Radin's experiments the subjects created a small doll in their own image and provided various objects (pictures, jewelry, an autobiography, and personally meaningful tokens) to "represent" them. They also gave a list of what makes them feel nurtured and comfortable. These and the accompanying information were used by the "healer" (who functioned analogously to the "sender" in thought- and image-transfer experiments) to create a sympathetic connection to the subject (the "patient"). The latter was wired up to monitor the activity of his or her autonomous nervous system—electrodermal activity, heart rate, blood pulse volume—and the healer was in an acoustically and electromagnetically shielded room in an adjacent building. The healer placed the doll and other small objects on the table in front of him and concentrated on them while sending randomly sequenced "nurturing" (active healing) and "rest" messages.

It turned out that the electrodermal activity of the patients, together with their heart rate, were significantly different during the active nurturing periods than during the rest periods, and blood pulse volume was significant for a few seconds during the nurturing period. Both heart rate and blood flow indicated a "relaxation response," which makes sense because the healer was attempting to "nurture" the subject via the doll. On the other hand, a higher rate of electrodermal activity showed that the patients' autonomic nervous system was becoming aroused. Why this should be so was puzzling until the experimenters realized that the healers nurtured the patients by rubbing the shoulders of the dolls that represented them or stroked their hair and face. This, apparently, had the effect of a "remote massage" on the patients.

Radin and colleagues concluded that the local actions and thoughts of the healer are mimicked in the remote patient almost as if healer and patient were next to each other. Distance between sender and receiver seems to make little difference. This was confirmed in a large number of trials by experimental parapsychologists William Braud and Marilyn Schlitz regarding the impact of the mental imagery of senders on the physiology of receivers. Braud and Schlitz found that the mental images of the sender could reach out over space to cause changes in the distant receiver. The effects are comparable to those that one's own mental processes produce on one's body. "Telesomatic" action by a distant person is similar to and nearly as effective as "psychosomatic" action by the subject on him- or herself.

This writer's decade long experience with remote-healer María Sági of the Koerbler Institute in Budapest, and with physician Gordon Flint of the Psionic Medical Society in the U.K., confirms a basic fact: some forms of transpersonal healing, from near or from far away, can effectively replace traditional medical treatment. An impressive number of rigorous studies on spiritual as well as distant healing at medical schools, experimental laboratories, and hospitals support this conclusion. At the request of patients, some healers have been allowed into British National Health Service hospitals since 1970, paid by the NHS itself. Psychiatrist Daniel Benor, founder of the UK's Doctor-Healer Network, examined more than 200 controlled trials of "spiritual healing," mainly of humans, but some directed at animals, plants, bacteria, yeasts, laboratory cell cultures, and enzymes. Nearly half had clearly documented therapeutic effects.

U.S. physician Larry Dossey speaks of a new era in medical practice. He calls it Era III, nonlocal medicine. It follows Era II, mind-body medicine, and Era I, standard biochemical medicine.

Although pockets of skepticism remain, on the whole the debate in scientific circles is shifting from *whether* transpersonal phenomena occur to *how* they occur. The experience of scores of transpersonal psychologists, consciousness researchers, and alternative medical practitioners furnishes evidence that such phenomena are real and occur on the level both of the brain and the mind, and the body and the environment.

The paradigm emerging in the sciences of consciousness is consistent with that which comes to the fore in the new physics and the new biology. It testifies that there is constant connection and communication among all the things that coexist and coevolve in the cosmos and in the biosphere—and that human consciousness is a part of the evolving web of connection and communication that envelops the planet.

The holistic paradigm in the sciences tells us that we are not machines, however complex and sophisticated. We are not truly separate from each other and from our planetary environment. We are participants in nature, interacting with each other, with the wide reaches of the biosphere, and with the still wider reaches of the universe.

The holistic insight of cutting-edge science supports and lends legitimacy to the Holos-consciousness emerging in society. Science can contribute to healing the split that separates one person from another, one people from other peoples, and all of humankind from Earth and the cosmos.

References & Further Reading

Artigiani, Robert, in Ervin Laszlo, Robert Artigiani, Allan Combs, and Vilmos Csányi, *Changing Visions: Human Cognitive Maps Past, Present, and Future*. Adamantine Press, London, 1996.

Benor, Daniel J., *Healing Research*, Vol. 1, Helix Editions, London, 1993.

———, *Healing Research: Holistic Energy Medicine and Spiritual Healing*. Helix Verlag, Munich 1993.

———, "Survey of spiritual healing research." *Contemporary Medical Research*, Vol. 4, 9 (1990).

Bohm, David, *Wholeness and the Implicate Order*. Routledge & Kegan Paul, London 1980.

Buks, E., R. Schuster, M. Heiblum, D. Mahalu, and V. Umansky, "Dephasing in electron interference by a 'which-path' detector." *Nature*, Vol. 391 (26 February 1998).

Braud, W., and M. Schlitz, "Psychokinetic influence on electrodermal activity," *Journal of Parapsychology*, Vol. 47 (1983).

Celente, Gerald, "Global Simplicity," *The Trends Journal*, Vol. VI, 1, Winter 1997.

Council for a Parliament of the World's Religions, *Towards a Global Ethic*. Chicago, 1993.

Crick, Francis, *The Astonishing Hypothesis*. Charles Scribner, New York, 1994.

"Cyber: Ricerche Olistiche (Nitamo Montecucco)," in *Cyber* (Milan), November 1992.

Davies, Paul, *God and the New Physics*. Simon & Schuster, New York, 1983.

———, and John Gribbin, *The Matter Myth*. Simon & Schuster, New York, 1992.

———, *The Mind of God*. Simon & Schuster, New York, 1992.

Dossey, Larry, *Recovering the Soul: A Scientific and Spiritual Search*. New York, Bantam 1989.

————, *Healing Words: The Power of Prayer and the Practice of Medicine*. Harper San Francisco, 1993.

Dürr, S., T. Nonn, and G. Rempe, "Origin of quantum-mechanical complementarity probed by a 'which-way' experiment in an atom interferometer." *Nature*, Vol. 395 (3 September 1998).

Elgin, Duane, *Global Consciousness Change: Indicators of an Emerging Paradigm*. Millennium Project, San Anselmo, CA. 1997.

————, *Awakening Earth: Exploring the Evolution of Human Culture and Consciousness*. Morrow, New York, 1993.

Elkin, A.P., *The Australian Aborigines*. Angus & Robertson, Sydney, 1942.

Environment Monitor, Health of the Planet Survey of International Environment Monitor Ltd. (IEML), Ottawa, 1997.

Giscard d'Estaing, Olivier, *Enterprise Ethique*. Le Cercle d'Ethique des Affaires, Paris, 1998.

Goodwin, Brian, "Development and evolution." *Journal of Theoretical Biology*, 97, 1982.

————, "Organisms and minds as organic forms." *Leonardo*, 22, 1 (1989).

Gore, Al, *Earth in the Balance*. Houghton Mifflin and Co., Boston, 1992.

Grinberg-Zylverbaum, Jacobo M. Delaflor, M. E. Sanchez-Arellano, M. A. Guevara, and M. Perez, "Human communication and the electrophysiological activity of the brain." *Subtle Energies*, Vol. 3,3 (1993).

Grof, Stanislav, *The Adventure of Self-Discovery*. State University of New York Press, Albany, 1988.

————, *The Cosmic Game*. State University of New York Press, Albany, 1998.

————, with Hal Zina Bennett, *The Holotropic Mind*. Harper San Francisco, 1993.

Hansen, G. M., M. Schlitz, and C. Tart, "Summary of remote viewing research," in Russell Targ and K. Harary, *The Mind Race*. 1972–1982. Villard, New York, 1984.

Haroche, Serge, "Entanglement, decoherence and the quantum/classical boundary." *Physics Today*, (July 1998).

Harvard Medical School, *The Impact of Belief on Medical Outcomes Examined*, 1997 (mimeo).

Ho, Mae Wan, *The Rainbow and the Worm: The Physics of Organisms*. World Scientific, Singapore and London, 1993.

————, "The physics of organisms and the naturalistic ethics of wholeness," in David Lorimer, Chris Clarke, John Cosh, Max Paye and Alan Mayne (eds.) *Wider Horizons: Explorations in Science and Human Experience*. The Scientific and Medical Network, Gibliston Mill, Scotland, 1999.

Honorton, C., R. Berger, M. Varvoglis, M. Quant, P. Derr, E. Schechter, and D. Ferrari, "Psi-communication in the Ganzfeld: Experiments with an automated testing system and a comparison with a meta-analysis of earlier studies." *Journal of Parapsychology*, 54 (1990).

Hoyle, Fred, *The Intelligent Universe*. Michael Joseph, London, 1983.

Human Development Report 1996. United Nations Development Programme. Mahbub ul Haq and Richard Jolly, principal coordinators. Oxford University Press, New York, 1996.

InterAction Council: *A Universal Declaration of Human Responsibilities*. 1 September 1997.

Laszlo, Ervin, *The Creative Cosmos*. Floris Books, Edinburgh, 1993.

———, *The Interconnected Universe*. World Scientific, Singapore and London, 1995.

———, *The Choice: Evolution or Extinction*. Tarcher/Putnam, New York, 1994.

———, *The Whispering Pond*. Element Books, Rockport, Shaftesbury and Brisbane, 1996.

———, *Evolution: The General Theory*. Hampton Press, Cresskill, NJ, 1997.

———, *The Systems View of the World*. Hampton Press, Cresskill, NJ, 1997.

———, *Cosmic Connections: The Physics and Metaphysics of Natural Coherence* (in press).

———, and Christopher Laszlo, *The Insight Edge: An Introduction to the Theory and Practice of Evolutionary Management*. Quorum Books, Westport, CT, 1997.

———, Stanislav Grof, and Peter Russell, *The Consciousness Revolution: A Transatlantic Dialogue*. Element Books, Shaftesbury and Boston, 1999.

Loye, David, (ed.) *The Evolutionary Outrider: The Impact of the Human Agent on Evolution*. Essays Honoring Ervin Laszlo. Fred Praeger, Westport, CN; Adamantine, London, 1998.

Nelson, John E., *Healing the Split*. State University of New York Press, Albany, 1994.

Netherton, Morris, and Nancy Shiffrin, *Past Lives Therapy*. William Morrow, New York, 1978.

Penrose, Roger, *The Emperor's New Mind*. Oxford University Press, New York, 1989.

Persinger, M. A., and S. Krippner, "Dream ESP experiments and geomagnetic activity." *Journal of the American Society for Psychical Research*, Vol. 83, 1989.

Puthoff, Harold A., "Source of vacuum electromagnetic zero-point energy." *Physical Review* A, 40.9 (1989).

————, and Russell Targ, "A perceptual channel for information transfer over kilometer distances: historical perspective and recent research." *Proceedings of the IEEE*, Vol. 64, 1976.

Ray, Paul H., "American Lives." *Noetics Sciences Review*, Spring 1996.

————, and Sherry Ruth Anderson, *The Cultural Creatives: How 50 Million People Are Changing the World*. Harmony Books, New York, 2000.

Reyner, J.H., George Laurence and Carl Upton, revised by Keith Suter, with Foreword by Ervin Laszlo, *Psionic Medicine*. C.W. Daniel, Saffron Walden, 2001.

Russell, Peter, *The Global Brain Awakens: Our New Evolutionary Leap*. Global Brain, Palo Alto, CA, 1995.

Targ, Russell, and Harold A. Puthoff, "Information transmission under conditions of sensory shielding," *Nature*, Vol. 251 (1974).

Targ, Russell, and K. Harary, *The Mind Race*. Villard Books, New York, 1984.

Tarnas, Richard, *The Passion of the Western Mind*. Ballantine Books, New York, 1993.

Tart, Charles, *States of Consciousness*. Dutton, New York, 1975.

Taylor, Alastair M. *Time-Space-Technics. The World Futures General Evolution Studies*, Vol. 16, Gordon & Breach, New York and London (in preparation).

Taylor, Angus, *Magpies, Monkeys, and Morals. What Philosophers Say about Animal Liberation*. Broadview Press, Peterborough, Ontario, 1999.

Ullman, M., and S. Krippner, *Dream Studies and Telepathy: An Experimental Approach*. Parapsychology Foundation, New York, 1970.

Varvoglis, Mario, "Goal-directed- and observer-dependent PK: An evaluation of the conformance-behavior model and the observation theories." *Journal of the American Society for Psychical Research*, 80 (1986).

Wackernagel, M., and J. D. Yount, "The ecological footprint: An indicator of progress toward regional sustainability." *Environmental Monitoring and Assessment* 51 (1998).

Woolger, Roger, *Other Lives, Other Selves*. Doubleday, New York, 1987.

World Wildlife Fund, Living Planet Report. WWF International, New Economics Foundation, and World Conservation Monitoring Centre Gland, London and Cambridge, 1998.

Index

About the Author

E RVIN LASZLO is the author or editor of sixty-nine books translated into as many as seventeen languages, and has over four hundred articles and research papers and six volumes of piano recordings to his credit. He serves as editor of the monthly *World Futures: The Journal of General Evolution* and of its associated *General Evolution Studies* book series.

Laszlo is generally recognized as the founder of systems philosophy and general evolution theory, serving as founder-director of the General Evolution Research Group and as past president of the International Society for the Systems Sciences. He is the recipient of the highest degree in philosophy and human sciences of the Sorbonne, the University of Paris, as well as of the Artist Diploma of the Franz Liszt Academy of Budapest. His numerous prizes and awards include four honorary doctorates.

Ervin Laszlo's unusual career spans music, philosophy, science, futures studies, and world affairs. Born in Budapest, Hungary in 1932, his talent for music was discovered at the age of five. At seven he was admitted to the Franz Liszt Academy under the wing of famed composer-conductor Ernst von Dohnanyi. His debut with the Budapest Philharmonic at the age of nine established him as one of the great child prodigies of the time. Following a hiatus of barely a year due to the siege of Budapest at the end of World War II, Laszlo embarked on an international music career highlighted by the Grand Prize of the International Music Competition of Geneva in 1947, and a New York recital debut a few months later. Just fifteen, he was hailed by New York critics as an artist who has few peers among pianists of any age. With major write-ups in *LIFE, Time, Newsweek*, and other national and international media, he settled in New York and traveled from there to tour the five continents.

In his late teens Laszlo's childhood interest, fostered by his philosopher uncle in Budapest, in questions about meaning in nature and life and destiny in society resurfaced. It prompted him to undertake systematic readings in these fields and to follow courses and seminars at New York's Columbia University and New School for Social Research. His copious notes accompanied him on his concert tours and in 1961 were the subject of a casual dinner conversation following a recital in The Hague. His dinner partner, who showed keen interest in his ideas, took the notes and reappeared the following morning with an offer to publish them — he turned out to be the philosophy editor of the renowned Dutch publishing house Martinus Nijhoff. The publication of these notes two years later marked a turning point in Laszlo's career. He was asked to join the University of Fribourg's Institute of East European Studies, and two books and numerous research papers later he received an invitation to spend a year at the Philosophy Department at Yale University.

Laszlo's professional involvement in science and philosophy followed a consistent if highly personal path. His main interest centered on the perennial "great questions" of science and philosophy, in particular the evolution of the cosmos, the nature and direction of the evolution of life and of consciousness, and the meaning of the changes and transformations we are witnessing today in culture and civilization. His initial 1963 book *Essential Society: An Ontological Reconstruction* was inspired by the metaphysics of Whitehead and was followed by *Beyond Scepticism and Realism*, a methodological treatise, and *Individualism, Collectivism and Political Power*, an analysis of the ideological divide in the postwar world. *La Metaphysique de Whitehead*, an application of Whitehead's "organic philosophy" to human society, served as Laszlo's thesis at the Sorbonne for the *Doctorat d'Etat ès-Lettres et Sciences Humaines*, completing his formal credentials in the academic world.

While at Yale Laszlo read von Bertalanffy's *General System Theory*, met von Bertalanffy, and began to elaborate *Introduction to Systems Philosophy*, the seminal work with which his name became thereafter associated. Appointments at various U.S. universities, including the State University of New York, led to a visiting semester at Princeton's Center of International Studies. His seminar at the Woodrow Wilson School on the systems approach to world order engaged the attention of Club of Rome founder Aurelio Peccei, who enlisted Laszlo to complement the economic and physical "outer limits" emphasis of the Club's first report, *The Limits to Growth*, with a human and cultural "inner limits" orientation. Laszlo's research resulted in 1977 in the publication of the voluminous *Goals for Mankind*, the third global report to The Club of Rome, as well as of the personal treatise, *The Inner Limits of Mankind*. To research these works, the executive director of the United Nations Institute for Training and Research (UNITAR) invited Laszlo as Special Fellow; an appointment that was followed by his being placed in charge of the Institute's work on the New International Economic Order. As program director, Laszlo spent seven years at U.N. headquarters in New York, producing fifteen volumes on the New International Economic Order and another six volumes on Regional and Interregional Cooperation.

Having completed these assignments in the mid-80s, Laszlo decided to take a sabbatical period before returning to his university. He moved to his converted medieval farmhouse in Tuscany in search of the peace and freedom to analyze his experience in the academic world and at the United Nations. He returned to his quest of researching answers to the great questions of evolution in our time. His *Evolution: The Grand Synthesis* was published in 1987 and was soon translated into Italian, German, Spanish, French, Chinese, and Portuguese. It was followed by the application of his evolutionary insights to contemporary society: *The Age of Bifurcation*. Inspiring considerable debate and discussion, it appeared in Russian and Turkish in addition to all of the previous languages.

Laszlo's reading and research at his Tuscan farmhouse was soon punctuated by frequent visits to the United States, Japan, China, and many parts of Europe, as the United Nations University, the newly formed European Culture Impact Research Consortium, and then Federico Mayor, the Director-General of UNESCO, sought his advice and collaboration. These activities culminated in 1993, when Laszlo, one of the two plenary speakers at the Third World Congress of the World Federation of Hungarians (the other being nuclear scientist Edward Teller), proposed that Hungary, neither a major economic nor a military power but a significant force in the fields of science, art, and culture, should be the host to an international "Artist's and Writer's Club" to complement the Club of Rome's insistence on economic and political measures with emphasis on the urgency of new thinking, better values, and a deeper sense of personal and professional responsibility. The Hungarian government responded with the offer to set up the secretariat of the worldwide organization that was to become known as the Club of Budapest.

Since the middle of the 1990s Laszlo has been dividing his time and energies between fundamental research in the new sciences—resulting in a series of books (*The Creative Cosmos*, 1993, *The Interconnected Universe*, 1995, and *The Whispering Pond*, 1996)—and building up the worldwide organization and activities of the Club. He produced the first report to the Club in 1997: *Third Millennium: The Challenge and the Vision*. The definitive enlarged and updated version of this report is now in the hands of the reader.

In addition to designing and overseeing the global projects of the Club of Budapest, including the annual awarding of the Planetary Consciousness Prizes and the celebration of the World Day of Planetary Consciousness (on March 20) and the World Day of Planetary Ethics (on September 22), Laszlo is currently completing two major science books, *Wholeness in Cosmos and Consciousness*, and the more popularly oriented *Holos: The Fabulous World of the New Sciences*.

About the Club of Budapest

T HE CLUB OF BUDAPEST is an informal association of creative people in diverse fields of art, literature, and the spiritual domains of culture. It is dedicated to the proposition that only by changing ourselves can we change our world—and that to change ourselves we need the kind of insight and perception that art, literature, and the domains of the spirit can best provide. The members of the Club of Budapest use their artistic creativity and spiritual insight to enhance awareness of global problems and human opportunities. They communicate their insights in word and image, in sound and motion, and in the myriad new media and technologies. They are recognized world leaders in their fields of literary, artistic, or spiritual activity; their names are assurance of insight, and their membership in the club a testimony of their dedication to our common future.

The Challenge and the Mission

The insight in view of which the Club of Budapest has been founded is that today's world is in rapid and fundamental transformation. This transformation is unfinished and as yet open. Thus, our future is not to be predicted; it must be created. The possibilities are vast, and the choice among them is ours. The new worlds we could create range from an inhuman world of frustration, conflict, and violence to a world of peace and equity, capable of offering conditions for personal fulfillment and social development. The world we will create in reality depends on us. It depends on the thinking, values, and perceptions of people in all walks of life, in all parts of the world. The alternative to a world governed "from above" can only be a self-governing world—one that chooses the shape of things to come "from within." The critical factor in the choice of our common destiny is the thinking, the valuing, and the perception of individuals: the shape of our consciousness.

Nobody can shape our consciousness but ourselves. To evolve the kind of consciousness that could ensure that our future is bright, we must apprehend our situation on this planet in all its dimensions—sense it with our heart and soul. In this regard the contribution of human culture and creativity is the important resource. Creative people in the spiritual domains, in literature, in the arts, in design, and in all spheres of innovative thinking and acting are the greatest resource of contemporary humanity. This resource cannot, must not, be left unharnessed in meeting the unparalleled challenge: to transform today's inequitable and unsustainable world into a humane and sustainable one.

The Club of Budapest is dedicated to the proposition that *the "revolution of consciousness" is perhaps the last, and certainly the best, hope of humankind.* The club is dedicated to harnessing the power of creativity of spiritual leaders, artists, writers, and innovators in all societies and spheres of activity to catalyze this peaceful and vital revolution in the shared interest of our generation and of generations to come.

The Manifesto of Planetary Consciousness*

A new way of thinking has become the necessary condition for responsible living and acting. Evolving it means fostering creativity in all people, in all parts of the world. Creativity is not a genetic but a cultural endowment of human beings. Culture and society

---

*Drafted by Ervin Laszlo in consultation with the Dalai Lama and adopted by the Club of Budapest on October 27, 1996.

change fast, while genes change slowly: no more than one half of one percent of the human genetic endowment is likely to alter in an entire century. Hence most of our genes date from the Stone Age or before; they could help us to live in the jungles of nature but not in the jungles of civilization. Today's economic, social, and technological environment is our own creation, and only the creativity of our mind—our culture, spirit, and consciousness—will enable us to cope with it. Genuine creativity does not remain paralyzed when faced with unusual and unexpected problems but confronts them openly, without prejudice. Cultivating it is a precondition of finding our way toward a globally interconnected society in which individuals, enterprises, states, and the whole family of peoples and nations could live together peacefully, cooperatively, and with mutual benefit.

A CALL FOR RESPONSIBILITY

In the course of the twentieth century, people in many parts of the world have become conscious of their rights as well as of many persistent violations of them. This development is important, but in itself it is not enough. We must now become conscious of the factor without which neither rights nor other values can be effectively safeguarded: our individual and collective *responsibilities*. We are not likely to grow into a peaceful and cooperative human family unless we become responsible social, economic, political, and cultural actors.

We human beings need more than food, water, and shelter; more even than remunerated work, self-esteem, and social acceptance. We also need something to live for: an ideal to achieve, a responsibility to accept. Because we are aware of the consequences of our actions, we can and must accept responsibility for them. Such responsibility goes deeper than many of us may think. In today's world all people, no matter where they live and what they do, have become responsible for their actions as:

- private individuals;
- citizens of a country;

- collaborators in business and the economy;
- members of the human community; and
- persons endowed with mind and consciousness.

As individuals, we are responsible for seeking our interests in harmony with, and not at the expense of, the interests and well-being of others; responsible for condemning and averting any form of killing and brutality; responsible for not bringing more children into the world than we truly need and can support; and for respecting the right to life, development, and equal status and dignity of all the children, women, and men who inhabit the Earth.

As citizens of our country, we are responsible for demanding that our leaders "beat swords into plowshares" and relate to other nations peacefully and in a spirit of cooperation; that they recognize the legitimate aspirations of all communities in the human family; and that they do not abuse sovereign powers to manipulate people and the environment for shortsighted and selfish ends.

As collaborators in business and actors in the economy, we are responsible for ensuring that corporate objectives do not center uniquely on profit and growth but include a concern that products and services respond to human needs and demands without harming people and impairing nature; that they do not serve destructive ends and unscrupulous designs; and that they respect the rights of all entrepreneurs and enterprises who compete fairly in the global marketplace.

As members of the human community, it is our responsibility to adopt a culture of nonviolence, solidarity, and economic, political, and social equality, promoting mutual understanding and respect among people and nations whether they are like us or different, demanding that all people everywhere should be empowered to respond to the challenges that face them with the material as well as spiritual resources that are required for this unprecedented task.

And *as persons endowed with mind and consciousness*, our responsibility is to encourage comprehension and appreciation for the excellence of the human spirit in all its manifestations, and for inspiring awe and wonder for a cosmos that brought forth life and consciousness and holds out the possibility of its continued evolution toward ever higher levels of insight, understanding, love, and compassion.

A Call for Planetary Consciousness

In most parts of the world the real potential of human beings is sadly underdeveloped. The way children are raised depresses their faculties for learning and creativity; the way young people experience the struggle for material survival results in frustration and resentment. In adults this leads to a variety of compensatory, addictive, and compulsive behaviors. The result is the persistence of social and political oppression, economic warfare, cultural intolerance, crime, and disregard for the environment.

Eliminating social and economic ills and frustrations calls for considerable socioeconomic development, and that is not possible without better education, information, and communication. These, however, are blocked by the absence of socioeconomic development, so that a vicious cycle is produced: underdevelopment creates frustration, and frustration, giving rise to defective behaviors, blocks development. This cycle must be broken at its point of greatest flexibility and that is the development of the spirit and consciousness of human beings. Achieving this objective does not preempt the need for socioeconomic development with all its financial and technical resources but calls for a parallel mission in the spiritual field. Unless people's spirit and consciousness evolve to the planetary dimension, the processes that stress the globalized society-nature system will intensify and create a shock wave that could jeopardize the entire transition toward a peaceful and cooperative global society. This would be a setback for humanity and a danger for everyone. Evolving human spirit and consciousness is the first vital cause shared by the whole of the human family.

Planetary consciousness is knowing as well as feeling the vital interdependence and essential oneness of humankind and the conscious adoption of the ethic and the ethos that this entails. Its evolution is the basic imperative of human survival on this planet.

Honorary Members

H.E. Dsingis Aitmatov, *writer*
H.E. Oscar Arias, *Statesman, Nobel Peace Laureate*
Dr. A.T. Ariyaratne, *Buddhist spiritual leader*
Maurice Béjart, *dancer/choreographer*
Prof. Thomas Berry, *theologian/scientist*
Sir Arthur C. Clarke, *writer*
H.H. The XIVth Dalai Lama, *statesman/spiritual leader*
Dr. Riane Eisler, *feminist historian/activist*
Milos Forman, *film director*
Peter Gabriel, *musician*
Dr. Jane Goodall, *scientist*
Rivka Golani, *musician*
H.E. Mikhail Gorbachev, *political leader*
H.E. Arpád Göncz, *writer/statesman*
Prof. Otto Herbert Hajek, *sculptor*
H.E. Václav Havel, *writer/statesman*
Pir Vilayat Inayat-Khan, *Sufi spiritual leader*
Miklós Jancsô, *film director*
Ken-Ichiro Kobayashi, *orchestra director*
Gidon Kremer, *musician*
Prof. Shu-Hsien Liu, *philosopher*
Eva Marton, *opera singer*
Zubin Mehta, *orchestra director*
Lord Yehudi Menuhin‡, *musician*
Dr. Edgar Mitchell, *scientist/astronaut*
Prof. Edgar Morin, *philosopher/sociologist*
Dr. Robert Muller, *educator/activist*
Prof. Nicholas Negroponte, *scientist, digital media leader*
Ute-Henriette Ohoven, *UNESCO ambassador*
Prof. Gillo Pontecorvo, *film director*
H.E. Ruiyyih Rabbani‡, *Baha'i spiritual leader*
Jean-Pierre Rampal‡, *musician*
Mary Robinson, *political and human rights leader*

Mstislav Rostropovich, *orchestra director*
Sir Josef Rotblat, *scientist/Nobel Peace Laureate*
Dr. Peter Russell, *philosopher/futurist*
H.E. Karan Singh, *statesman, Hindu spiritual leader*
Sir George Solti‡, *orchestra director*
Sir Sigmund Sternberg, *interfaith spiritual leader*
Liv Ullmann, *film actor/director*
Sir Peter Ustinov, *actor/writer/director*
H.E. Vigdis Finnbogadottir, *political leader*
H.E. Richard von Weizsäcker, *statesman*
Prof. Elie Wiesel, *writer/Nobel Peace Laureate*
Betty Williams, *activist/Nobel Peace Laureate*
Prof. Mohammed Yunus, *economist/financial leader*

Note: ‡ indicates that the individual is deceased.

The Secretariat

THE INTERNATIONAL ORGANIZATION

FOUNDER/PRESIDENT:
Ervin Laszlo, Montescudaio, Italy and Budapest, Hungary

HONORARY PRESIDENT:
Sir Peter Ustinov, Bursins, Switzerland

GLOBAL AMBASSADOR:
Lady Fiona Montagu, Beaulieu, England

SECRETARY-GENERAL:
Thomas Druyen, Düsseldorf, Germany

VICE PRESIDENTS:

ORGANIZATIONAL DEVELOPMENT:
Helga Breuninger, Stuttgart, Germany

PLANETARY CONSCIOUSNESS PERSONALITIES:
Danièle Thoma, Cologne, Germany

PUBLIC AND HUMAN RELATIONS:
Thomas Heidenreich, Düsseldorf, Germany

FINANCE:
Edgar Walterscheidt, Düsseldorf, Germany

MANAGING DIRECTORS:

PLANETARY CONSCIOUSNESS EDUCATION:
David Lorimer, Colinburgh, Fife, Scotland

PLANETARY CONSCIOUSNESS PROJECTS:
Peter Spiegel, Stuttgart, Germany

PLANETARY BUSINESS ETHICS:
Christopher Laszlo, Great Falls, VA

PLANETARY VISION FESTIVAL:
David Woolfson, Toronto, Canada

COORDINATORS:

ACTIVITY COORDINATOR:
Miriam Holbe, Düsseldorf, Germany

NETWORK COORDINATOR:
Gregorio Rivera, Monterrey, Mexico

ADVISOR
David Lawrence, Mill Valley, CA

THE NATIONAL CLUBS

PRESIDENT, CLUB OF BUDAPEST FOUNDATION, GERMANY:
Thomas Druyen, Düsseldorf, Germany

PRESIDENT, CLUB OF BUDAPEST USA:
Muriel Adcock, San Francisco, USA

COORDINATOR, CLUB OF BUDAPEST MEXICO:
Gregorio Rivera, Monterrey, Mexico

PRESIDENT, CLUB OF BUDAPEST BRAZIL:
Tamas Makray, São Paulo, Brazil

PRESIDENT, CLUB OF BUDAPEST FRANCE:
Yves Fisselier, Paris

PRESIDENT, CLUB OF BUDAPEST ITALY:
Nitamo Montecucco, Bagni di Lucca and Florence

COORDINATOR, CLUB OF BUDAPEST AUSTRIA:
Gerhard Schweter, Vienna, Austria

PRESIDENT, CLUB OF BUDAPEST FOUNDATION, HUNGARY:
Ervin Laszlo, Montescudaio, Italy, and Budapest, Hungary
    PROGRAM DIRECTOR: Mária Sági, Budapest, Hungary

PRESIDENT, CLUB OF BUDAPEST INDIA:
Karan Singh, New Delhi, India

PRESIDENT, CLUB OF BUDAPEST CHINA:
Min Jiayin, Beijing, PRC

COORDINATOR, CLUB OF BUDAPEST JAPAN:
Shigeyuki Itow, Fukuoka, Japan

PRESIDENT, CLUB OF BUDAPEST SAMOA:
Marco Kappenberger, Apia, Samoa

* * * * * * * *

THE CLUB OF BUDAPEST FOUNDATION, HUNGARY
Szentháromság-tér 6
1014 Budapest, Hungary,
TEL/FAX: +36-1-375-1885
E-MAIL: Budapest_Club@matavnet.hu

THE CLUB OF BUDAPEST INTERNATIONAL FOUNDATION
Schloss Garath, Garather Schlossallee 19
40595 Düsseldorf, Germany
TEL: +49-211-9708-132, FAX: -131
E-MAIL: welcome@club-of-budapest.de

INTERNET: www.club-of-budapest.org